Bogey-Free Retirement

HOW TO AVOID THE BIG NUMBER IN RETIREMENT

H. Marcus "Mark" Witt
Jordan M. Witt, CRPC
Witt Financial Group

Copyright © 2023 by Mark Witt and Jordan Witt.

All rights reserved. No part of this publication may be reproduced, distributed, or transmitted in any form or by any means, including photocopying, recording, or other electronic or mechanical methods, without the prior written permission of the publisher, except in the case of brief quotations embodied in critical reviews and certain other noncommercial uses permitted by copyright law. For permission requests, write to the publisher at the address below. These materials are provided to you by Mark Witt and Jordan Witt for informational purposes only and Mark Witt, Jordan Witt and Advisors Excel LLC expressly disclaim any and all liability arising out of or relating to your use of same. The provision of these materials does not constitute legal or investment advice and does not establish an attorney-client relationship between you, Mark Witt, and Jordan Witt. No tax advice is contained in these materials. You are solely responsible for ensuring the accuracy and completeness of all materials as well as the compliance, validity, and enforceability of all materials under any applicable law. The strategies found within may not be suitable for every situation. You are expressly advised to consult with a qualified attorney or other professional in making any such determination and to determine your legal or financial needs. No warranty of any kind, implied, expressed, or statutory, including but not limited to the warranties of title and non-infringement of third-party rights, is given with respect to this publication.

Mark Witt and Jordan Witt/Witt Financial Group LLC
91 Hwy 70 E, Suite 102
Crossville, TN 38555
www.wittfinancialgroup.com

Book layout ©2023 Advisors Excel LLC

Bogey-Free Retirement/ Mark Witt and Jordan Witt — 1st edition

ISBN 9798852862723

Witt Financial Group LLC (WFG) is an independent financial services firm that helps individuals create retirement strategies using a variety of investment and insurance products to custom suit their needs and objectives.

Investment advisory services are offered through Witt Financial Group LLC (WFG), a state-registered investment advisor located in Tennessee. WFG may only provide advisory services to individuals residing in Tennessee, Florida, or other jurisdictions where WFG is exempt from registration. Insurance products and services are offered separately through licensed and appointed agents. WFG does not provide specific tax or legal advice and all individuals are encouraged to contact their tax or legal professional before taking any actions.

The contents of this book are provided for informational purposes only and are not intended to serve as the basis for any financial decisions. Any tax, legal, or estate planning information is general in nature. It should not be construed as legal or tax advice. Always consult an attorney or tax professional regarding the applicability of this information to your unique situation.

Information presented is believed to be factual and up-to-date, but we do not guarantee its accuracy, and it should not be regarded as a complete analysis of the subjects discussed. All expressions of opinion are those of the authors as of the date of publication and are subject to change. Content should not be construed as personalized investment advice nor should it be interpreted as an offer to buy or sell any securities mentioned. A financial advisor should be consulted before implementing any of the strategies presented.

Investing involves risk, including the potential loss of principal. No investment strategy can guarantee a profit or protect against loss in periods of declining values. Any references to protection benefits or guaranteed/lifetime income streams refer only to fixed insurance products, not securities or investment products. Insurance and annuity product guarantees are backed by the financial strength and claims-paying ability of the issuing insurance company.

Examples in this book include purely hypothetical scenarios and many of the examples are based on actual client situations that Witt Financial Group has encountered. Of course, all names have been changed and all are detailed here only as examples and should not be deemed as specific investment recommendations or advice.

"Golf is deceptively simple and endlessly complicated; it satisfies the soul and frustrates the intellect. It is at the same time rewarding and maddening—and it is without a doubt the greatest game mankind has ever invented."

~ Arnold Palmer

Hobert F. Witt and Mary Lou Witt, parents to Mark and grandparents to Jordan, were instrumental in the writing of this book. Thank you for instilling your Christian values in both of us.

Table of Contents

The Importance of Planning i

Longevity 1

Taxes 23

Market Volatility 31

Retirement Income 39

Social Security 55

401(k)s & IRAs 69

Annuities 81

Estate & Legacy 89

Why Retirement is Different for Women 97

Finding a Financial Professional 105

About the Authors 111

PREFACE
The Importance of Planning

Ricky Gregg was nothing short of a child prodigy.
His dad, Ronnie, put a golf club in his hands at the age of seven. Little did Ronnie know that his son would accomplish so much in this wonderful game of golf.

A year later, Ricky was honing his skills at a par three course in Knoxville, Tennessee. By the time he was ten, Ricky was playing with his grandfather, Gilbert Knott, and his father Ronnie at Bays Mountain Country Club.

By the age of twelve, Ricky was beating his father and grandfather. Ronnie knew his son had a special gift. At the age of thirteen, he shot a sixty-five at Bays Mountain. From the ages of thirteen to eighteen, he won the club championship there each year.

Ricky was destined for greatness. He was a star player for Young High School in Knoxville and was heavily recruited before choosing to play collegiate golf at the University of Tennessee.

In his career, he won over seventy-five golf tournaments as an amateur and three as a professional. At the University of Tennessee, he was named team MVP in 1976, 1977, and 1978. He was named to the All-SEC team those same three years. He is the only UT golfer to receive an invitation to play in the NCAA tournament three times. He was the Tennessee Amateur of the Year in 1977, played in three U.S. Amateurs and played in the 1977 U.S. Open at Southern Hills Country Club in Tulsa, Oklahoma. Ricky was inducted into the Knoxville Sports Hall of Fame in 2008 and is a member of the University of Tennessee Hall of Fame Class of 2016.

Ricky attempted to achieve his ultimate dream of being a professional golfer on the PGA Tour multiple times. On his sixth and what turned out to be his final attempt at qualifying—or "Q-School"—Ricky missed earning his tour card by a single stroke.

At the age of twenty-seven, Ricky was faced with the toughest decision of his life: continue pursuing his dream of being a professional golfer or get a job. Once again, his father Ronnie was there to help. He pointed Ricky toward a tremendous opportunity and today Ricky is a successful businessman.

At every stage of his professional journey, one thing stayed consistent for Ricky: the planning and strategy had to change at each level to maximize his opportunities for success.

What was true for Ricky in golf is also true when it comes to planning for retirement. You have to be able to adapt to make the most of this next chapter of your life.

A lot of people who come in to meet with us at Witt Financial Group have enjoyed success. Maybe they've saved a lot of money, accumulated plenty in the stock market to retire, or even have a number in mind that will allow them to achieve their goals after they have stopped working.

But what we so often tell people is that what worked to this point may not be the best strategy in the next phase of life.

While accumulation is typically the goal in your working years, the shift to preservation can be just as important in retirement. That may seem like a small change, but it can make a tremendous difference. A memorable experience for Ricky helps illustrate our point.

When Ricky was aiming to qualify for the PGA Tour at Q-School in Orlando, Florida, he suddenly went on a cold streak.

"I must have shanked twenty in a row," he said, "and 'shank' is the most dreaded word in golf. I was panicking."

Two days before Q-School, a friend set him up for a meeting with golfing legend Arnold Palmer. It took one stroke for Arnold to declare Ricky had a "pitch-out" problem. (Notice he didn't call it a "shank." Amazing how the mind of an all-time great works.)

Arnold laid an empty ball sleeve box on the outside of Ricky's ball and explained the pitch-out was a result of an over-the-top swing with a closed club face. Ricky took a swing that hit the sleeve, and Arnold instructed him to take the club straight back and bring it through without hitting the small box.

Ricky gradually progressed and began to drive the ball straight without any shanks. Arnold worked with him for over an hour to iron out the kinks, and when they were done, he wished Ricky luck, reminding him to be mentally tough.

The next week at Q-School, Ricky shot twelve-under over eight rounds with no pitch-outs, and from that one session, developed a lifelong friendship with his golf hero.

A lot of people—whether it's preparing for a golf tournament or retirement—think they can handle problems all on their own. Before meeting Arnold, Ricky was already All-SEC at the University of Tennessee. But that bout with the shanks was something he'd never personally encountered.

Meanwhile, Arnold had been around the game long enough that he'd seen dozens suffer from the same issue.

While Mark and Jordan never met the legendary Arnold Palmer, they are fortunate to call Ricky a close friend.

"When he told us the story of how 'the King' fixed his game, we were on the edge of our seats, not just because of Arnold's generosity and expertise, but because it resembled so closely the guidance we aim to provide our clients who are on the course to retirement," Mark said. "We have helped enough people to quickly determine whether they're on track for a 'bogey-free retirement' or if they've got a 'pitch-out' problem that needs to be addressed."

Witt Financial Group is led by a father-son team with decades of experience. Mark, the firm's founder and president, has spent nearly twenty-five years as a financial professional, and Jordan entered the financial services field after graduating from East Tennessee State University in 2011.

In golf, you can hit the ball in a water hazard, take a drop, and still manage par. A mistake in retirement planning can be much less forgiving. You only get one shot to do this right, which is why we titled our book *Bogey-Free Retirement*.

Professional golfers carry yardage books detailing specifics of the course they are playing. A yardage book has comprehensive diagrams of every hole, including all the hazards, bunkers, distances, slopes, and tiers. Simply put, a yardage book is a guide to help you navigate the course. That's why we have developed *The Bogey-Free Retirement Yardage Book* to help you navigate the five major areas of retirement planning:

1. Income: For a secure retirement, you must have predictable retirement income sources *with the goal of beating inflation.*
2. Investments: Investing *for* retirement is vastly different than investing *in* retirement. Making your money last requires a totally different set of disciplines.
3. Taxes: As Americans, we should strive to legally pay the least amount of taxes possible. "Pay the IRS what you owe, but do not leave a tip."
4. Health Care: Some may think a market crash is the most costly thing that can happen to a retiree, but the rising cost of long-term health care could prove far more devastating to a family than a temporary market correction.
5. Legacy: Your personalized estate plan is a strategy to ensure your assets are distributed to your loved ones according to your wishes in a timely and tax-efficient fashion.

Our motto is, "Hope for the best; plan for the worst." Everything in life is not perfect. Things will happen that we don't expect, both good and bad. So, let's plan for both.

The Bogey-Free Retirement Process starts with a strategy meeting to discover someone's dreams and desires. Then we discuss each of the five areas mentioned above. After that, we review and analyze their investment portfolio. Finally, we make recommendations based on our findings that are in the best interest of the client. If necessary, we can refer people to a tax professional or an estate planning attorney. Our goal is for a retiree to have complete financial confidence throughout retirement.

A person with a retirement plan has a much higher chance of success than one without. Many people spend more time planning their family vacation than their retirement. Retirement planning is too important to neglect.

Why not take a few hours of your time, meet with a suitable advisor, and put together your *Bogey-Free Retirement* plan? In the time it takes to play a round of golf, you can make great strides toward your retirement peace of mind!

CHAPTER 1

Longevity

You would think the prospect of the grave would loom more frightening as we age, yet many retirees say their number one concern is actually running out of money in their twilight years.[1] Unfortunately, this fear is justified in part because of one significant factor: We're living longer.

According to the Social Security Administration, in 1950, the average life expectancy for a sixty-five-year-old man was seventy-eight, and the average for a sixty-five-year-old woman was eighty-one. In the 2022 Trustees Report issued by the SSA, those averages were eighty-three and eighty-five, respectively.[2]

The bottom line of many retirees' budget woes comes down to this: They just didn't plan to live so long. Now, when we are younger and in our working years, that's not something we necessarily see as a bad thing; don't some people fantasize about living forever or, at least, reaching the ripe old age of one hundred?

However, with a longer lifespan, as we near retirement, we face a few snags. Our resources are finite—we only have so much money to provide income—but our lifespans can be unpredictably long, perhaps longer than our resources allow.

---

[1] Liz Weston. nerdwallet.com. March 25, 2021. "Will You Really Run Out of Money in Retirement?"
https://www.nerdwallet.com/article/finance/will-you-really-run-out-of-money-in-retirement
[2] Social Security Administration. 2022 Trustees Report. "Actuarial Life Table." https://www.ssa.gov/oact/STATS/table4c6.html

Also, longer lives don't necessarily equate with healthier lives. The longer you live, the more money you will likely need to spend on health care, even excluding long-term care needs like nursing homes.

You will also run into inflation. If you don't plan to live another twenty-five years but end up doing so, inflation at an average of 3 percent will approximately double the price of goods over that time period. Put a harsh twist on that and the buying power of a ninety-year-old will be half of what they possessed if they retired at sixty-five.[3]

Because we don't necessarily get to have our cake and eat it, too, our collective increased longevity hasn't necessarily increased the healthy years of our lives. Typically, our life-extending care most widely applies to the time in our lives where we will need more care in general. Think of common situations like a pacemaker at eighty-five, or cancer treatment at seventy-eight.

"Wow, Mark and Jordan," we can hear you say, "way to start with the good news first."

We know, we've painted a grim picture, but all we're concerned about here is cost. It's hard to put a dollar sign on life, but that is essentially what we're talking about when discussing longevity and finances. Living longer isn't a bad thing; it just costs more, and one key to a sound retirement strategy is preparing for it in advance.

Many investors tend to focus on short-term performance, but we believe it's more important to focus on a disciplined long-term approach with our investments to account for these longer lifespans. We currently have clients who are over the age of ninety. By establishing a disciplined long-term plan many years ago, they still have assets and income remaining. We recently spoke to a client, age ninety-three. He's a retired business owner who has been with us for twenty years. By

---

[3] Bob Sullivan, Benjamin Curry. Forbes. April 28, 2021. "Inflation And Retirement Investments: What You Need to Know."
https://www.forbes.com/advisor/retirement/inflation-retirement-investments/

employing strategies that emphasized protection as well as long-term growth, he has maintained a great standard of living.

Unfortunately, we have seen dear clients pass away in the past few years, some of whom were in their nineties. They had sufficient income to enjoy their lifestyle and were still able to leave money to their children, grandchildren, and charity. We like to design plans that allow people to potentially spend more in the early retirement years (such as their sixties and seventies) while still having ample funds to provide what they need if they live to age ninety or beyond.

A retiree typically spends more money on traveling and entertainment in their earlier years. We have clients who don't plan to spend much in their early retirement years, but we may encourage them to do so. If you've worked thirty or forty years, take some time to enjoy retirement. No one knows how long retirement will actually last.

This is why we emphasize income planning for today and tomorrow, investment planning with an eye on beating inflation, and contingency plans for future escalating health care expenditures.

Some people we work with prioritize leaving a legacy for loved ones. Others have a different goal. We once met a couple in their mid-seventies. Their plan was to live a healthy life and then, on her ninetieth birthday, go to her favorite restaurant, enjoy a meal, go home, kiss each other good night, and pass away peacefully in their sleep. Meanwhile, the check they wrote to the restaurant bounced, because they had spent their last dollar on their last day on Earth. Talk about timing things perfectly!

We worked with one couple, whom we'll call Bob and Sue. They were high school sweethearts who married soon after graduation. They were hard-working people who lived in the Midwest. Bob was a social worker, and Sue worked as a registered nurse. They raised three children. They valued faith, family, and hard work. Their lifestyle wasn't opulent, but they had a wonderful life. They saved and invested for the future. They were the definition of long-term investors. They dreamed of the day they would retire and enjoy their golden years together. Their children were all successful in their own right—obviously, great parenting was the key!

Bob and Sue began to search for the perfect retirement spot. That led them to Crossville, which you may know is the "Golf Capital of Tennessee." They purchased property there and drew plans for their dream retirement home (i.e., their forever home). They were so excited about their new life and their new home.

However, a few short months after they retired and relocated to Tennessee, Bob developed a serious illness. Within a few months, he passed away. Sue was now in a new location, and the love of her life was not around to enjoy it with her.

Sue was not familiar with how their investments aligned with their retirement goals. Her husband had handled all the family finances. All this turmoil happened in 2008, the year of the Great Recession. Bob was not there for Sue to consult about the family finances. Meanwhile, their broker simply said, "Don't worry; the market always comes back." And while that statement may be true, Sue—all alone and unfamiliar with the investment and planning process—had just suffered massive investment losses and was so worried that she couldn't sleep at night. Sue was unprepared for the chaos surrounding market declines, so she sought a second opinion.

We met with Sue several times and collaborated on a new strategy that was specifically designed to meet her goals and objectives, not just on a financial level but an emotional one as well. Everyone's situation is different, but one major point we have stressed to Sue and others is that investing *for* retirement is different than investing *in* retirement. It's a different set of rules and disciplines.

I spoke with Sue recently. She is doing well and most likely will live into her nineties. She misses Bob every day, but celebrates life surrounded by family and friends. By addressing longevity along with her financial needs, Sue is well-positioned to enjoy whatever life brings!

Retiring Early

A key part of planning for retirement revolves around retirement income. After all, retirement is cutting the cord that tethers you to your employer and your monthly check. However, that check often comes with many other benefits, particularly health care. Health care is often the thing that can unexpectedly put dreams for an early retirement on hold. Some employers offer health benefits to their retired workers, but that number has declined drastically over the past several decades. In 1988, among employers who offered health benefits to their workers, 66 percent offered health benefits to their retirees. In 2022, that number was 21 percent of large firms.[4]

So, with employer-offered retirement health benefits on the wane, this becomes a major point of concern for anyone who is looking to retire—particularly those who are looking to retire before age sixty-five, when they would become eligible for Medicare coverage. Fidelity estimates that the average retired couple at age sixty-five will need approximately $315,000 for medical expenses, not including long-term care.[5] Do you think it's likely that cost will decrease?

Even if you are working until age sixty-five or have plans to cover your health expenses until that point, we often have clients who incorrectly assume Medicare is their golden ticket to cover all expenses. That is simply not the case.

---

[4] Henry J. Kaiser Family Foundation. October 27, 2022. "2022 Employer Health Benefits Survey Section Eleven: Retiree Health Benefits." https://www.kff.org/report-section/ehbs-2022-section-11-retiree-health-benefits/

[5] Fidelity Viewpoints. Fidelity. August 29, 2022. "How to Plan for Rising Health Care Costs." https://www.fidelity.com/viewpoints/personal-finance/plan-for-rising-health-care-costs

Retiring Later

Planning for a long life in retirement partly depends on when you retire. While many people end up retiring earlier than they anticipated (due to injuries, layoffs, family crises, and other unforeseen circumstances), continuing to work past age sixty (and even sixty-five) is still a viable option for others and can be an excellent way to help establish financial comfort in retirement.

There are many reasons for this. For one, you obviously still earn a paycheck and the benefits accompanying it. Medical coverage and beefing up your retirement accounts with further savings can be significant by themselves but continuing your income should also keep you from dipping into your retirement funds, further allowing them the opportunity to grow.

Additionally, for many workers, their nine-to-five job is more than just clocking in and out. Having a sense of purpose can keep us active physically, mentally, and socially. That kind of activity and level of engagement may also help stave off many of the health problems that plague retirees. Avoiding a sedentary life is one of the advantages of staying plugged into the workforce, if possible.

You hear about people going back to work after retiring. Most don't do so because they need the money. Instead, they work to stay physically and mentally sharp. Socialization also inspires some to work again.

We love the game of golf, but for many, playing golf every day in retirement gets old. We have clients who retired from full-time jobs and then went back to work part-time because they missed the social and competitive aspects of working.

On the flip side, we have clients who worked well into their seventies and wish they had retired earlier. Staying sharp in retirement is great, but you can have a healthy balance of work and fun. At the end of the day, we want our clients to have a "work-optional" lifestyle. This means they can work if they so desire, but they do not have to work to maintain a comfortable retirement. Work consumes over half of our lives. Consider what is most important to you and create a retirement plan that gives you this work-optional lifestyle. The factors you should consider when deciding to retire or work longer are your happiness, health, and dreams.

When Derek and Kim—a couple in their late fifties—retired, his goal was to play golf every day. He loved the game and lowered his handicap to the low single digits. She was active in the community and involved in various charities and organizations. They did it right, invested properly, and retired early to live out their dreams.

However, a couple of years later, Derek felt a need to do something more. Yes, he still loved golf, but he needed a purpose. He kept coming back to Proverbs 29:18: "Where there is no vision, the people perish." He needed a vision—a purpose. Thankfully, he found a ministry in his church where he could help mentor young couples on marriage and parenting skills. Since then, Kim has joined Derek in the couple's ministry while still being active in her charities and organizations.

Derek still plays golf two or three times a week, and his handicap is still in single digits. Now, though, he has a renewed purpose for life. They both now say it's the happiest they have ever been.

Health Care

Take a second to reflect on your health care plan. Although working up to or even past age sixty-five would allow you to avoid a coverage gap between your working years and Medicare, that may not be an option for you. Even if it is, when you retire, you will need to make some decisions about what kind of insurance coverage you may need to supplement your Medicare. Are there any medical needs you have that may require coverage in addition to Medicare? Did your parents or grandparents have any inheritable medical conditions you might consider using a special savings plan to cover?

These are all questions that are important to review with your financial professional so you can be sure you have enough money put aside for health care.

Health care expenditures could be the most devastating aspect to your retirement—physically, emotionally, and financially. The idea of long-term care insurance is relatively new to our society, as people now live longer thanks to better health care, healthier lifestyles, and advanced medical technology.

The majority of retirees have insurance in case of catastrophic losses due to an automobile accident or a fire in their homes. Home and auto insurance are easy to comprehend, and many people have had claims in the past. However, if you polled people over the age of sixty-five and asked how many believe they will spend time in a nursing home, very few would say they expect to. They just think it will not happen to them. However, it's essential to plan for it, because nursing home costs could be the most devastating financial loss ever incurred by a family. As the old saying goes, it's better to have it (insurance) and not need it, than need it and not have it.

The best thing you can do for yourself is to scope out the health care field early, compare costs often, and prepare for out-of-pocket costs well in advance—decades, if possible.

Long-Term Care

Longevity means the need for long-term care is statistically more likely to happen. If you intend to pass on a legacy, planning for long-term care is paramount, since most estimates project nearly 70 percent of Americans will need some type of it.[6] However, this may be one of the biggest and most stressful

---

[6] Richard W. Johnson. urban.org. June 24, 2021. "What is the Lifetime Risk of Needing and Receiving Long-Term Services and Supports?" https://www.urban.org/research/publication/what-lifetime-risk-needing-and-receiving-long-term-services-and-supports

pieces of longevity planning we encounter in our work. For one thing, who wants to talk about the point in their lives when they may feel the most limited? Who wants to dwell on what will happen if they no longer can toilet, bathe, dress, or feed themselves?

We get it; this is a less-than-fun part of planning. But a little bit of preparation now can go a long way!

When it comes to your longevity, just like with your goals, one of the important things to do is sit and dream. It may not be the fun, "road-trip-to-the-Grand-Canyon" kind of dreaming, but you can spend time envisioning how you want your twilight years to look.

For instance, if it is important for you to live in your home for as long as possible, who will provide for the day-to-day fixes and to-dos of housework if you become ill? Will you set aside money for a service, or do you have relatives or friends nearby whom you could comfortably allow to help you? Do you prefer in-home care over a nursing home or assisted living? This could be a good time to discuss the possibility of moving into a retirement community versus staying where you are, or whether it's worth moving to another state and leaving relatives behind.

These are all important factors to discuss with your spouse and children, as *now* is the right time to address questions and concerns. For instance, is aging in place more important to one spouse than the other? Are the friends or relatives who live nearby emotionally, physically, and financially capable of helping you for a time if you face an illness?

Many families we meet with find these conversations very uncomfortable, particularly when children discuss nursing home care with their parents. A knee-jerk reaction for many is to promise they will care for their aging parents. This is noble and well-intentioned, but there needs to be an element of realism here. Does "help" from an adult child mean they stop by and help you with laundry, cooking, home maintenance, and bills? Or does it mean they move you into their spare room when you have hip surgery? Are they prepared to help you use the restroom and bathe if that becomes difficult for you to do on your own?

We don't mean to discourage families from caring for their own; this can be a profoundly admirable relationship when it works out. However, we've seen families put off planning for late-in-life care based on a tenuous promise that the adult children would care for their parents, only to watch as the support system crumbles. Sometimes this is because the assumed caregiver hasn't given serious thought to the preparation they would need, both in a formal sense and regarding their personal physical, emotional, and financial commitments. This is often also because we can't see the future: Alzheimer's disease and other maladies of old age can exact a heavy toll. When a loved one reaches the point where he or she is at risk of wandering away or needs help with two or more activities of daily living, it can be more than one person or family can realistically handle.

If you know what you want, communicate with your family about both the best-case and worst-case scenarios. Then, hope for the best, and plan for the worst.

Realistic Cost of Care

Wrapped up in your planning should be a consideration for the cost of long-term care. One study estimates that by 2030, the nation's long-term care costs could reach $2,500,000,000,000 ($2.5 *trillion*) as roughly twenty-four million Americans require some type of long-term care.[7] The potential costs for such care and treatment can be underestimated, especially by those who have maintained robust health and find it difficult to envision future declines to their condition.

Another piece of planning for long-term care costs is anticipating inflation. It's common knowledge that prices have

---

[7] Tara O'Neill Hayes, Sara Kurtovic. Americanactionforum.org. February 18, 2020. "The Ballooning Costs of Long-Term Care." https://www.americanactionforum.org/research/the-ballooning-costs-of-long-term-care/

been and keep rising, which can lower your purchasing power on everything from food to medical care. Long-term care is a big piece of the inflation-disparity pie.

While local costs vary from state to state, here's the national median for various forms of long-term care (plus projections that account for a 3 percent annual inflation, so you can see what we are referencing):[8]

	Long-Term Care Costs: Inflation			
	Home Health Care, Homemaker Services	Adult Day Care	Assisted Living	Nursing Home (semi-private room)
Annual 2021	$59,488	$20,280	$54,000	$94,900
Annual 2031	$79,947	$27,255	$72,571	$127,538
Annual 2041	$107,442	$36,628	$97,530	$171,400
Annual 2051	$144,393	$49,225	$131,072	$230,347

Fund Your Long-Term Care

One crucial mistake we see are those who haven't planned for long-term care because they assume the government will provide everything. But that's a big misconception. The government has two health insurance programs: Medicare and Medicaid. These can greatly assist you in your health care needs in retirement but usually don't provide enough coverage to

---

[8] Genworth Financial. June 2022. "Cost of Care Survey 2022." https://www.genworth.com/aging-and-you/finances/cost-of-care.html

cover all your health care costs in retirement. Our firm isn't a government outpost, so we don't get to make decisions when it comes to forming policy and specifics about either one of these programs. We're going to give an overview of both, but if you want to dive into the details of these programs, you can visit www.Medicare.gov and www.Medicaid.gov.

Medicare

Medicare covers those aged sixty-five and older and those who are disabled. Medicare's coverage of any nursing home related health issues is limited. It might cover your nursing home stay if it is not a "custodial" stay, and it isn't long-term. For example, if you break a bone or suffer a stroke, stay in a nursing home for rehabilitative care, and then return home, Medicare may cover you. But, if you have developed dementia or are looking to move to a nursing facility because you can no longer bathe, dress, toilet, feed yourself, or take care of your hygiene, etc., then Medicare is not going to pay for your nursing home costs.[9]

You can enroll in Medicare anytime during the three months before and three months after your sixty-fifth birthday. Miss your enrollment deadline, and you could risk paying increased premiums for the rest of your life.[10] On top of prompt enrollment, there are a few other things to think about when it comes to Medicare, not least among them being the need to understand the different "parts," what they do, and what they don't cover.

Part A

Medicare Part A is what you might think of as "classic" Medicare. Hospital care, some types of home health care, and

---

[9] Medicare.gov. "What Part A covers." https://www.medicare.gov/what-medicare-covers/part-a/what-part-a-covers.html
[10] Medicare.gov. "When can I sign up for Medicare?" https://www.medicare.gov/basics/get-started-with-medicare/sign-up/when-can-i-sign-up-for-medicare

major medical care fall under this. While most enrollees pay nothing for this service (as they likely paid into the system for at least ten years), you may end up paying, either based on work history or delayed signup. In 2023, the highest premium is $506 per month, and a hospital stay has a deductible of $1,600.[11] And if you have a hospital stay that surpasses sixty days, you could be looking at additional costs; keep in mind, Medicare doesn't pay for long-term care and services.

Part B

Medicare Part B is an essential piece of wrap-around coverage for Medicare Part A. It helps pay for doctor visits and outpatient services. This also comes with a price tag: Although the Part B deductible is only $226 in 2023, you will still pay 20 percent of all costs after that, with no limit on out-of-pocket expenses. The Part B monthly premium for 2023 ranges from the standard amount of $164.90 to $560.50.[12]

Part C

Medicare Part C, more commonly known as Medicare Advantage plans, are an alternative to a combination of Parts A, B, and sometimes D. Administered through private insurance companies, these have a variety of costs and restrictions, and they are subject to the specific policies and rules of the issuing carrier.

Part D

Medicare Part D is also through a private insurer and is supplemental to Parts A and B, as its primary purpose is to

---

[11] Medicare. "Medicare 2023 Costs at a Glance."
https://www.medicare.gov/your-medicare-costs/medicare-costs-at-a-glance
[12] Ibid.

cover prescription drugs. Like any private insurance plan, Part D has its quirks and rules that vary from insurer to insurer.

The Donut Hole

Even with a Part D plan in place, you may still have a coverage gap between what your Part D private drug insurance pays for your prescription and what basic Medicare pays. In 2023, the coverage gap is $4,660, which means that after you meet your private prescription insurance limit, you will spend no more than 25 percent of your drug costs out-of-pocket before Medicare will kick in to pay for more prescription drugs.[13]

Medicare Supplements

Medicare Supplement Insurance, MedSup, Medigap, or plans labeled Medicare Part F, G, H, I, J . . . Known by a variety of monikers, this is just a fancy way of saying "medical coverage for those over sixty-five that picks up the tab for whatever the federal Medicare program(s) doesn't." Again, costs, limitations, etc., vary by carrier.

Does that sound like a bunch of government alphabet soup to you? It certainly does to us. And did you read the fine print? Unpredictable costs, varied restrictions, difficult-to-compare benefits, donut holes, and coverage gaps. That's par for the course with health care plans throughout our adult lives. What gives? Medicare was supposed to be easier, comprehensive, and at no cost!

The truth is there is probably no stage of life when health care is easy to understand.

According to the Fidelity Retiree Health Care cost estimate, an average retired couple aged sixty-five in 2022 may need approximately $315,000 saved (after tax) to cover health care

---

[13] Medicare. "Costs in the coverage gap." https://www.medicare.gov/drug-coverage-part-d/costs-for-medicare-drug-coverage/costs-in-the-coverage-gap

expenses in retirement.[14] This is a massive figure which continues to get higher every year with the rising cost of health care and inflation.

Medicaid

Medicaid is a program the states administer, so funding, protocol, and limitations vary. Compared to Medicare, Medicaid more widely covers nursing home care, but it targets a different demographic: those with low incomes.

If you have more assets than the Medicaid limit in your state and need nursing home care, you will need to use those assets to pay for your care. You will also have a list of additional state-approved ways to spend some of these assets over the Medicaid limit, such as pre-purchasing burial plots and funeral expenses or paying off debts. After that, your remaining assets fund your nursing home stay until they are gone, at which point Medicaid will jump in.

Some people aren't stymied by this, thinking they will just pass on their financial assets early, gifting them to relatives, friends, and causes so they can qualify for Medicaid when they need it. However, to prevent this exact scenario, Uncle Sam has implemented the look-back period. Currently, if you enroll in Medicaid, you are subject to having the government scrutinize the last five years of your finances for large gifts or expenses that may subject you to penalties, temporarily making you ineligible for Medicaid coverage.

So if you're planning to preserve your money for future generations and retain control of your financial resources during your lifetime, you'll probably want to prepare for the costs of longevity beyond a "government plan."

---

[14] Fidelity Investments. May 16, 2022. "Fidelity Releases 2022 Retiree Health Care Cost Estimate: 65-Year-Old Couple Retiring Today Will Need an Average of $315,000 for Medical Expenses."

Self-Funding

One way to fund a longer life is the old-fashioned way, through self-funding. There are a variety of financial tools you can use, and they all have their pros and cons. If your assets are in low-interest financial vehicles (savings, bonds, CDs), you risk letting inflation erode the value of your dollar. Or, if you are relying on the stock market, you have more growth potential, but you'll also want to consider the possible implications of market volatility. What if your assets take a hit? If you suffer a loss in your retirement portfolio in early or mid-retirement, you might have the option to "tighten your belt," so to speak, and cut back on discretionary spending to allow your portfolio the room to bounce back. However, if you are retired and depend on income from a stock account that just hit a downward stride, what are you going to do?

HSAs

These days, you might also be able to self-fund through a health savings account (or HSA) if you have access to one through a high-deductible health plan (you will not qualify to save in an HSA after enrolling in Medicare). In an HSA, any growth of your tax-deductible contributions will be tax-free, and any distributions paid out for qualified health costs are also tax-free. Long-term care expenses count as health costs, so if this is an option available to you, it is one way to use the tax advantages to self-fund your longevity. Bear in mind, if you are younger than sixty-five, any money you use for nonqualified expenses will be subject to taxes and penalties, and if you are older than sixty-five, any HSA money you use for non-medical expenses is subject to income tax.

LTCI

One slightly more nuanced way to pay for longevity, specifically for long-term care, is long-term care insurance, or LTCI. As car insurance protects your assets in case of a car accident and home insurance protects your assets in case something happens to your house, long-term care insurance aims to protect your assets in case you need long-term care in an at-home or nursing home situation.

As with other types of insurance, you will pay a monthly or annual premium in exchange for an insurance company paying for long-term care down the road. Typically, policies cover two to three years of care, which is adequate for an "average" situation: it's estimated 70 percent of Americans will need about three years of long-term care of some kind.

Now, there are a few oft-cited components of LTCI that make it unattractive for some:

- Expense — LTCI can be expensive. It is generally less expensive the younger you are, but a sixty-five-year-old couple who purchased LTCI in 2022 could expect to pay a combined amount of $3,750 each year for an average three-year coverage policy. And the annual cost only increases from there the older you are.[15]
- Limited options — Let's face it: LTCI may be expensive for consumers, but it can also be expensive for companies that offer it. With fewer companies willing to take on that expense, this narrows the market, meaning opportunities to price shop for policies with different options or custom benefits are limited.
- If you know you need it, you might not be able to get it. Insurance companies offering LTCI are taking on a risk that you may need LTCI. That risk is the foundation of the product—you may or may not need it. If you know you will need it because you have a dementia diagnosis or another illness for which you will need long-term care, you will likely not qualify for LTCI coverage.

---

[15] American Association for Long-Term Care Insurance. 2023. . "Long-Term Care Insurance Facts – Data – Statistics – 2022 Reports" https://www.aaltci.org/long-term-care-insurance/learning-center/ltcfacts-2022.php#2022costs-65

- Use it or lose it—If you have LTCI and are in the minority of Americans who die having never needed long-term care, all the money you paid into your LTCI policy is gone.
- Possibly fluctuating rates—Your rate is not locked in on LTCI. Companies maintain the ability to raise or lower your premium amounts. This means some seniors face an ultimatum: Keep funding a policy at what might be a less affordable rate *or* lose coverage and let go of all the money they paid in so far.

After that, you might be thinking, "How can people possibly be interested in LTCI?" But let us repeat ourselves—as many as 70 percent of Americans will need long-term care. And, although only one in ten Americans aged fifty-five-plus have purchased LTCI, keep in mind the high cost of nursing home care. Can you afford $9,034 a month to put into nursing home care and still have enough left over to protect your legacy? This is a very real concern considering one set of statistics reported a two-in-three chance that a senior citizen will become physically or cognitively impaired in their lifetime.[16] So, not to sound like a broken record, but it is vitally important to have a plan in place to deal with longevity and long-term care if you intend to leave a financial legacy.

Health care planning is one of the five key pillars of *Bogey-Free Retirement*. We believe it's our job to discuss options and solutions to offset rising health care costs. While it is a conversation many are reluctant to have, long-term health care must ultimately be funded in one of three ways:

1. You can **assume** the risk and pay all costs out of pocket.
2. You can **assign** the risk by purchasing life insurance, LTCI or a hybrid insurance policy.

---

[16] payingforseniorcare.com. 2022. "Long-Term Senior Care Statistics" https://www.payingforseniorcare.com/statistics

3. You can **ignore** the risk and ultimately endure government assistance if and when your funds are exhausted.

A few relevant statistics to keep in mind:
- The longer you live, the more likely you are to continue living; the longer you live, the more health care you will likely need to pay for.
- The average cost of a private nursing home room in the United States in 2021 was $9,034 a month.[17] But keep in mind, that is just the nursing home—it doesn't include other medical costs, let alone pleasantries like entertainment or hobby spending.
- In 2022, Fidelity calculated that a healthy couple retiring at age sixty-five could expect to pay around $315,000 over the course of retirement to cover health and medical expenses.[18]

We know. "Whoa, there, Mark and Jordan, I was hoping to have a realistic idea of health costs, not be driven over by a cement mixer!"

The good news is, while we don't know these exact costs in advance, we know there *will* be costs. And you won't have to pay your total Medicare lifetime premiums in one day as a lump sum. Now that you have a good idea of health care costs in retirement, you can *plan* for them! That's the real point here: Planning in advance can keep you from feeling nickel-and-dimed to your wits' end (no pun intended!). Instead, having a sizeable portion of your assets earmarked for health care can allow you the freedom to choose health care networks, coverage

---

[17] Genworth Financial. January 31, 2022. "Genworth 2020 Cost of Care Survey." https://www.genworth.com/aging-and-you/finances/cost-of-care.html
[18] Fidelity Viewpoints. Fidelity. August 29, 2022. "How to Plan for Rising Health Care Costs." https://www.fidelity.com/viewpoints/personal-finance/plan-for-rising-health-care-costs

options, and long-term care possibilities you like and that you think offer you the best in life.

Product Riders

LTCI and self-funding are not the only ways to plan for the expenses of longevity. Some companies are getting creative with their products, particularly insurance companies. One way they are retooling to meet people's needs is through optional product riders on annuities and life insurance.

One annuity rider some companies offer is a long-term care rider. If you have an annuity with a long-term care rider and are not in need of long-term care, your contract behaves as any annuity contract would—nothing changes. Generally speaking, if you reach a point when you can't perform multiple functions of daily life on your own, you notify the insurance company and a representative will turn on those provisions of your contract.

Like LTCI, different companies and products offer different options. Some annuity long-term care riders offer coverage of two years in a nursing home situation. Others cap expenses at two times the original annuity's value. It greatly depends. Some people prefer this option because there isn't a "use-it-or-lose-it" piece; if you die without ever having needed long-term care, you will still have had the income benefit from the base contract. Of course, as with any annuity or insurance contract, there are the usual restrictions and limitations. Withdrawing money from the contract will affect future income payments, early distributions can result in a penalty, income taxes may apply, and because the insurance company's solvency is what guarantees your payments, it's important to do your research about the insurance company you are considering purchasing a contract from.

Understandably, a discussion on long-term care is bound to feel at least a little tedious. Yet this is a critical piece of planning for income in retirement, particularly if you want to leave a legacy.

A family member told us the following story: Richard and Jan raised four children and owned the local hardware store in town. None of the children wanted to take over the family business, so Richard and Jan sold it. When they retired, their estate—including their residence—was valued at $1,500,000. Richard enjoyed retirement for several years before battling a chronic disease and ultimately succumbing to death. Then, Jan grew ill several years later. The family sold the house to prepare for her future medical needs. Her needs progressed from part-time care at home to finally being admitted to a nursing home for full-time care. Jan later developed dementia and was eventually diagnosed with Alzheimer's disease. She spent over a decade in a nursing home and her funds were exhausted.

When Jan was declared broke by the state, she went on Medicaid assistance. Sadly, she died just a few months later, leaving very little behind for her four children.

The children had urged their mother and father to purchase long-term care protection earlier in life, to which the father said, "That won't happen to us." Most families believe that things like this do not happen to them, but sadly, it's more common than you may think.

Something to ponder: If you own a home valued at $1,000,000, would you fully insure it? Likewise, if you have a $1,000,000 estate, should you consider insuring it?

Spousal Planning

Here's one thing to keep in mind no matter how you plan to save: Many of us will be planning for more than ourselves. Look back at all the stats on health events and the likelihood of long life and long-term care. If they hold true for a single individual, then the likelihood of having a costly health or long-term care event is even higher for a married couple. You'll be planning for not just one life, but two. So when it comes to long-term care insurance, annuities, self-funding, or whatever strategy you are looking at using, be sure you are funding longevity for the both of you.

CHAPTER 2

Taxes

Where to begin with taxes? Perhaps by acknowledging we all bear responsibility for the resources we share. Roads, bridges, schools . . . It is the patriotic duty of every American to pay their fair share of taxes. Many would agree with this sentiment. However, while they don't mind paying their fair share, they're not interested in paying one cent more than that!

Now, just talking taxes probably takes your mind to April—tax season. You are probably thinking about all the forms you collect and how you file. Perhaps you are thinking about your certified public accountant or another qualified tax professional and saying to yourself, "I've already got taxes taken care of, thanks!"

However, what we see when people come into our office is that their relationship with their tax professional is purely a January through April relationship. That means they may have a tax professional, but not a tax *planner*.

What we mean is tax planning extends beyond filing taxes. In April, we are required to settle our accounts with the IRS to make sure we have paid up on our bill or to even the score if we have overpaid. But real tax planning is about making each financial move in a way that allows you to keep the most money in your pocket and out of Uncle Sam's.

Now, as a caveat, we want to emphasize we are neither CPAs nor tax planners, but we see the way taxes affect our clients, and we want to assist our clients in implementing tax-efficient strategies in their retirement plans in conjunction with their tax professionals.

As we're writing this book in 2023, it's a great time for tax planning. The current tax rates expire on December 31, 2025. Will tax rates go up or down? No one knows, but we do know the rates change periodically, so it's important to plan for any outcome.

It is especially important to us to help our clients develop tax-efficient strategies in their retirement plans because each dollar they can keep in their pockets is a dollar we can put to work.

Let's say someone retires with $1,000,000 in their IRA or 401(k). That looks great on paper, but did you know they don't actually have $1,000,000? When we tell people this, they look at us like, "What?"

All qualified plans have a lien on them, and that lien is income taxes. Most people think all the money in a qualified plan is <u>THEIRS</u>. Not so fast; a portion actually belongs to <u>THE IRS</u>! It's often said, "Your IRA is an IOU to the IRS."

Imagine three buckets labeled "forever taxed," "later taxed," and "never taxed." We believe it's important to have money in all these buckets. Examples of "forever taxed" could be dividends and interest. "Later taxed" could be an IRA, 401(k), or deferred annuity. "Never taxed" could be a Roth IRA or life insurance policy. If you have money in an IRA/401(k) and think taxes will rise in the future, it may be wise to explore options for moving money from later-taxed accounts to never-taxed accounts.

When is the best time to plan for taxes? Yesterday. When is the next best time? Right now, because taxes will always be changing, and based on our national debt, they're likely to rise sometime in the future.

A strategic move to consider would be taking money from IRAs/401(k)s before the Required Minimum Distribution (RMD) age of seventy-three and to pay the tax now, possibly at a lower rate. Another strategic move would be to consider converting an old traditional IRA to a new Roth IRA. Again, paying the tax up front could result in long-term tax savings.

It's interesting to note that all five pillars of *Bogey-Free Retirement* are interrelated. Take income planning and tax planning, for example. Assume someone wants an income of $100,000 from their qualified plans. If they are in a 20 percent tax bracket, they must withdraw $125,000 from their qualified plan to net their desired income of $100,000. Income must be predictable and cover expenses. Investment planning should be designed for long-term growth and future income. Tax efficiency is vital. The havoc caused by long-term health care needs to be addressed, and legacy planning ensures your wealth is distributed among your loved ones as intended.

The Fed

Now, in the United States, taxes can be a rather uncertain proposition. Depending on who is in the White House and which party controls Congress, we might be tempted to assume tax rates could either decline or increase in the next four to eight years accordingly. However, there is one (large!) factor we, as a nation, must confront: the national debt.

Currently, according to USDebtClock.org, we are over $31,000,000,000,000 in debt and climbing. That's $31 *trillion* with a "T." With just $1 trillion, you could park it in the bank at a 0 percent interest rate and spend more than $54,000,000 every day for fifty years without hitting a zero balance.

Even if Congress got a handle and stopped that debt from its daily compound, divided by each taxpayer, we each would owe about $246,000, per USDebtClock.org. So, will that be check, cash, or Venmo?

The point here isn't to give you anxiety. We're just cautioning you that even with the rosiest of outlooks on our personal income tax rates, none of us should count on low tax rates for the long term. Instead, you and your network of professionals (tax, legal, and financial) should constantly be looking for ways to take advantage of tax-saving opportunities as they come. After all, the best "luck" is when proper planning meets opportunity.

So, how can we get started?

Know Your Limits

One of the foundational pieces of tax planning is knowing what tax bracket you are in, based on your income after subtracting pre-tax or untaxed assets. Your income taxes are based on your taxable income.

One reason to know your taxable income and your income tax rate is so you can see how far away you are from the next lower or higher tax bracket. This is particularly important when it comes to decisions such as gifting and Roth IRA rollovers.

For instance, when confronting the 2022 federal income tax return they filed in 2023, Mallory and Ralph's taxable income is just over $345,000, putting them in the 32 percent tax bracket and about $4,900 above the upper end of the 24 percent tax bracket. They have already maxed out their retirement funds' tax-exempt contributions for the year. Their daughter, Gloria, is a sophomore in college. This couple could shave a considerable amount off their tax bill if they use the $4,900 to help Gloria out with groceries and school—something they were likely to do anyway, but can now be deliberately put to work for them in their overall financial strategy.

Now, we use Mallory and Ralph only as an example—your circumstances are probably different—but we think this nicely illustrates the way planning ahead for taxes can save you money.

Assuming a Lower Tax Rate

Many people anticipate being in a lower tax bracket in retirement. It makes sense: You won't be contributing to retirement funds; you'll be drawing from them. And you won't have all those work expenses—work clothes, transportation, lunch meetings, etc.

Yet do you really plan on changing your lifestyle after retirement? Do you plan to cut down on the number of times you eat out, scale back vacations, and skimp on travel?

What we see in our office is many couples spend more in the first few years—or maybe the first decade—of retirement. Sure, that may taper off later on, but usually only just in time for their budget to be hit with greater health and long-term care expenses. Do you see where this is going? Many people plan as though their taxable income will be lower in retirement and are surprised when the tax bills come in and look more or less the same as they used to. It's better to plan for the worst and hope for the best, wouldn't you agree?

401(k)/IRA

One sometimes unexpected piece of tax planning in retirement concerns your 401(k) or IRA. Most of us have one of these accounts or an equivalent. Throughout our working lives we pay in, dutifully socking away a portion of our earnings in these tax-deferred accounts. There's the rub: tax-deferred, not tax-free. Very rarely is anything free of taxation when you get down to it. Using 401(k)s and IRAs in retirement is no different. The taxes the government deferred when you were in your working years are now coming due, and you will pay taxes on that income at whatever your current tax rate is.

Just to ensure Uncle Sam gets his due, the government also has a required minimum distribution (or RMD) rule. Beginning at age seventy-three, you are required to withdraw a certain minimum amount every year from your 401(k) or IRA, or else you will face a tax penalty on any RMD monies you should have withdrawn but didn't—and that's on top of income tax. The SECURE Act 2.0 reduced the penalty to 25 percent (from 50 percent). Timely corrections also can reduce the penalty to 10 percent.[19]

Of course, there is also the Roth account. You can think of the difference between a Roth and a traditional retirement account as the difference between taxing the seed and taxing the harvest. Because Roths are funded with post-tax dollars, there aren't tax penalties for early withdrawals of the principal. There are also no taxes on the growth after you reach age fifty-nine-and-one-half. Perhaps best of all, there are no RMDs. Of course, you must own a Roth account for a minimum of five years before you are able to take advantage of all its features.

This is one more area where it pays to be aware of your tax bracket. Some people may find it advantageous to "convert" their traditional retirement account funds to Roth account funds in a year during which they are in a lower tax bracket.[20] Others may opt to put any excess RMDs from their traditional retirement accounts into other products, like stocks or insurance.

Does that make your head spin? Understandable. That's why it's so important to work with a financial professional and tax planner who can help you execute these sorts of tax-efficient strategies and help you understand what you are doing and why.

Tax planning is one of the most ignored areas of financial planning. It is not the job of the IRS to tell you how to lower your taxes—it's your job. If you don't know how, you need to find a tax professional who does.

Let's say a family has investable assets of $1,000,000 and $600,000 is in qualified plans, such as an IRA or 401(k). At a 20 percent tax rate on the qualified assets, the family would owe the IRS $120,000 in taxes. The family has three options:

1. They can pay taxes each year they take a distribution and be subject to the prevailing tax rates. For many,

---

[19] Jim Probasco. Investopedia. January 6, 2023. "SECURE 2.0 Act of 2022." https://www.investopedia.com/secure-2-0-definition-5225115.
[20] Note: Before considering a Roth conversion, you should seek advice from a competent accountant or CPA.

this will be their ultimate plan. However, if you went to a banker to borrow money and they said, "I won't tell you the interest rate now; we'll figure it out later"—would you find that acceptable? No, you would want to know the rate from the start because the banker could increase the rate later. Same with Uncle Sam. He could charge an exorbitant rate in the future.

2. They could consider a Roth IRA conversion. Suppose you believed taxes were going up in the future. Would it be wise to consider taking an old IRA, paying the taxes now and converting it to a new Roth IRA (i.e., moving "later taxed" money to "never taxed")? Once, a lady mentioned to me that by converting her old IRA to a new Roth IRA, she was designing her own LTCI strategy. Essentially, those tax-free dollars with no RMD requirement—having grown for decades—would pay her potential nursing home bills. And if she did not require long-term health care, the money could be distributed tax free to her heirs. Brilliant!

3. They could consider withdrawing from the IRA, paying the tax, and purchasing a life insurance policy. Assuming the distribution was not needed for expenses, nor was it going to be given away or gifted, a properly structured life insurance policy is a strategy intended to create wealth for your heirs. The death benefit of the life insurance could eventually be used to pay the taxes due on the IRA, leaving the full remaining value of the IRA for your loved ones. Keep in mind: You must pass the health questionnaire to qualify for life insurance.

> *"Anyone may arrange his affairs so that his taxes shall be as low as possible; he is not bound to choose that pattern which best pays the treasury. There is not even a patriotic duty to increase one's taxes. Over and over again the Courts have said that there is nothing sinister in so arranging affairs as to keep taxes as low as possible. Everyone does it, rich and poor alike and all do right, for nobody owes any public duty to pay more than the law demands."*
>
> **— *Learned Hand***

CHAPTER 3
Market Volatility

Up and down. Roller coaster. Merry-go-round. Bulls and bears. Peak-to-trough.

Sound familiar? This is the language we use to talk about the stock market. With volatility and spikes, even our language is jarring, bracing, and vivid.

Still, financial strategies tend to revolve around market-based products, for good reasons. For one thing, there is no other asset class that packs the same potential for growth, pound for pound, as stock-based products. Because of growth potential, inflation protection, and new opportunities, it may be unwise to avoid the market entirely.

However, along with the potential for growth is the potential for loss. At the time this book was written, many are still feeling uneasy because of the economic fallout of the COVID-19 outbreak of 2020, followed by the economic downturn and the inflation spike that happened in 2022.

In his book *Secrets of Closing the Sale*, Zig Ziglar wrote, "The fear of loss is greater than the desire for gain." By studying investor behavior during times of market turbulence, people will either *respond* or *react*. When markets rise, people *respond* positively and stay the course. When markets fall, people *react* and become fearful, oftentimes making unwise decisions.

So how do we balance these factors? How do we try to satisfy both the need for protection and the need for growth?

For one thing, it is important to recognize the value of diversification. Now, we're not just talking about the diversification of assets among different kinds of stocks and bonds. That's only one kind of diversification; stocks and bonds, though different, are both still important market-based products. Most market-based products, even within a diversified portfolio, tend to rise or decline as a whole, just like an incoming tide. Therefore, a portfolio diversified in only market-sourced products won't automatically protect your assets during times when the market declines.

In addition to the sort of "horizontal diversification" you have by purchasing a variety of stocks and bonds from different companies, we also suggest you think about "vertical diversification" among asset classes. This means having different product types, including securities products, bank products, and insurance products—with varying levels of growth potential, liquidity, and protection—all in accordance with your unique situation, goals, and needs.

We're advocates of investing in global markets. But we realize that market risk isn't for everyone. We have clients with mixes of assets that range from conservative to aggressive. Risk can mean opportunity to some, fear to others. Assigning risk to an investor by asking a few questions on a cookie-cutter questionnaire or merely asking, "Are you a conservative investor or an aggressive investor?" is not appropriate today. The word "conservative" could mean entirely different things to a client and an advisor.

We have access to portfolio analytics and research that can provide cost-cutting advice that considers both short-term market changes and long-term client goals. Gone are the days of having to stereotype investors based on subjective terms such as "conservative" or "aggressive." The analytics show what would happen in a time like 2008 (the Great Recession), March 2020 (when COVID tanked the markets), or 2021 (when markets were positive). It's an enlightening experience for someone to see data expressed, not only in percentage gain or loss, but in real dollar gain or loss.

Investors have to shift their mindset once they are retired. Investing *for* retirement is much different than investing *in* retirement. Investing for retirement is fairly easy. You earn money and invest for long-term growth. Time is on your side. You are contributing in the *accumulation* phase. In retirement, you are in the *decumulation* phase. You are drawing down your assets. Taxes, inflation, and market risk take center stage. Time is not on your side.

We believe in advanced planning, and risk is one major component of planning. This is why, in our discovery meeting, we want to know about the person's experiences with investing in the past, such as what they like or don't like, their understanding of markets and investing, their risk tolerance, and their asset base and debt, if any. We want to know everything about their finances in order to make a good recommendation.

Behavioral finance is the study of psychological influences on investors and financial markets. It uses experiments and research to demonstrate that humans are not always rational regarding fluctuations in the stock market, and their decision-making is often flawed. Behavioral finance touches on the academic and emotional side of investing.

It's one thing if someone thinks they'd be fine weathering the storm and maintaining their plan even if the market declines 30 percent. But when markets actually do decline (and they will), the emotional stress causes many to make the wrong decision at the wrong time. A financial advisor needs to be able to guide investors during good and bad times.

Suppose a client wants to sell during a market decline; nothing has changed in their lifestyle, and nothing should cause them to make a change. In that case, it is the responsibility of the advisor to advise against such a move, even if it could mean the end of the relationship. A good advisor will tell clients what they need to hear, which isn't always what they want to hear.

> *"The stock market is a device for transferring money from the impatient to the patient."*
>
> *-Warren Buffett*

"Fairways and Greens"

There's an old adage in golf called "fairways and greens." If you hit every fairway and every green, you're going to shoot a low score. When you're looking at the overall diversification of your portfolio, part of the "fairways and greens" approach is knowing which products fit in what category: what has liquidity, what has protection, and what has growth potential.

Liquidity

We typically recommend having at least six months' to a year's worth of expenses in liquid assets. We don't need a lot of growth potential; they just need to be readily available when we need them. Think of a short, 100-yard par three with no danger. Liquidity includes assets like:

- Cash
- Money market accounts

Protection

Protection is the direction we like to see people generally move toward as they're nearing retirement. In this category, we're not looking for market returns or liquidity. We're looking for the safety of an insurance company, bank, or government entity. Think of laying up on every par five, regardless of the circumstances. Eliminate the big number and settle for par. This category includes products such as:

- Certificates of deposit (backed by banks)
- Government-based bonds (backed by the U.S. government)
- Life insurance (backed by insurance companies)
- Annuities (backed by insurance companies)

Growth

Growth is the category where the greatest opportunities exist, but also the greatest opportunity for risk. Think of a 220-yard shot to a par five, all carry over water. It could go either way. Examples of growth products include:
- Stocks
- Bonds
- Mutual funds
- Real estate investment trusts
- Alternative investments
- High-yield bonds

Our approach is backed by years of academic research. We believe in free markets and focusing on years in the markets, not days. We must embrace volatility because we can't avoid risk when investing in the markets. In the long term, they always recover, but in the short term, it can be painful. Markets reward patient investors. The worst days on Wall Street are often followed by the best days.

We prefer to use managed portfolios with a structured approach. We believe diversification is the key to building an appropriate risk/reward strategy. We can diversify between U.S. and international markets. We can choose developed markets and emerging markets. Our portfolio may contain large-cap, mid-cap, and small-cap stocks, and the portfolio can include both growth and value stocks.

Bonds can also be highly diversified between short duration, intermediate duration, and long-term duration, as well as between investment grade and high yield. Bonds can also be U.S. and international, as well as government and corporate.

When you invest in the market, you are investing in the companies, the ideas, the innovations, and the technologies that surround us on a day-to-day basis. The products and services provided by public companies around the globe improve our lives. In our opinion, there's no better place to put your money than helping the free market provide the tools to improve lives.

Dollar-Cost Averaging

With 401(k)s and other market-based retirement products, dollar-cost averaging is a concept that can work in your favor when you are investing for the long term. When the market is trending up, if you are consistently paying in money, month over month, great; your investments can grow, and you are adding to your assets. When the market takes a dip, no problem; your dollars buy more shares at a lower price. At some point, we hope the market will rebound, in which case your shares can grow and possibly be more valuable than they were before. This concept is what we call "dollar-cost averaging." While it can't ensure a profit or guarantee against losses, it's a time-tested strategy for investing in a volatile market.

However, when you are in retirement, this strategy may work against you. You may have heard of "reverse" dollar-cost averaging. Before, when the market lost ground, you were "bargain-shopping"; your dollars purchased more assets at a reduced price. When you are in retirement, you are no longer the purchaser; you are selling. So, in a down market, you have to sell more assets to make the same amount of money as what you made in a favorable market.

We've had lots of people step into our office to talk to us about this, emphasizing, "My advisor says the market always bounces back, and I have to just hold on for the long term."

There's some basis for this thinking; thus far, the market has always rebounded to higher heights than before. But this is no guarantee, and the prospect of potentially higher returns in five years may not be very helpful in retirement if you are relying on the income from those returns to pay this month's electric bill, for example.

People often ask us, "I bet your phone rings off the hook when the Dow drops 1,000 points in a single day, doesn't it?" The answer to this is occasionally, but not that often.

We start with an established plan for our clients. Addressing volatility starts with building a solid plan, just like building a house. We need a solid foundation (protection strategies), then walls (moderate risk), and lastly, a roof (long-term growth). We like the term "all-weather portfolio." In good times, it performs well. In bad times, it has levels of protection built in to help combat volatility for when—not if—it occurs.

One of the pillars of *Bogey-Free Retirement* is to ask questions designed to elicit a response regarding risk tolerance. Some of these questions are easy, while others may be quite uncomfortable. If we ask, "Is a 20 percent return okay?" then the answer is, "Yes." But if we ask, "Is it okay if the same portfolio could fall by 20 percent in a bad year?" then the answer could be, "Absolutely not," in which case, we must redesign the plan. On the other hand, the answer could be, "Sure, no problem." Then we would press the issue and say, "If your $1,000,000 portfolio fell 20 percent to $800,000 during a market decline, would you *respond* by sticking to your plan or *react* by abandoning your plan?" This is where we need the person to be honest and tell us their true feelings. We need that honesty to develop a *Bogey-Free Retirement* the client can be comfortable with throughout the inevitable ups and downs of the market.

Is There a "Perfect" Product?

To bring us back around to the discussion of liquidity, protection, and growth, the ideal product would be a "ten" in all three categories, right? Completely guaranteed, doubling in size every few years, and accessible whenever you want. Does such a product exist? Absolutely not.

Instead of running in circles looking for that perfect product—the silver bullet, the unicorn of financial strategies—it's more important to circle back to the concept of a balanced, asset-diverse portfolio.

This is why your interests may be best served when you work with a trusted financial professional who knows what various financial products can do and how to use them in your personal retirement strategy.

CHAPTER 4

Retirement Income

Retirement. For many of us, it's what we've saved for and dreamed of, pinning our hopes to a magical someday. Is that someday full of traveling? Is it filled with grandkids? Gardening? Maybe your fondest dream is simply never having to work again, never having to clock in or be accountable to someone else.

We put a lot of time into saving and investing our money for retirement—and even imagining what we want to do once we're retired—but we don't spend nearly as much effort developing a strategy for withdrawing those assets once we retire. Developing a retirement strategy is similar to planning a mountain trek: How we get down from the peak is just as important as how we got up there. Your strategy for the descent should be slow and steady—the same way you accumulated those assets. Climbers use a rope-and-pully system to control how quickly they rappel down a mountain. Likewise, at retirement you need the right tools and predetermined route to help protect assets and draw them down in a controlled yet flexible manner, with the ability to make course changes as necessary. Accumulating enough money is just half the journey. The other half is making that money last as long as you do.

Your ability to live a *Bogey-Free Retirement* all hinges on *income*. Without the money to support these dreams, even a basic level of work-free lifestyle is unsustainable. That's why planning for your income in retirement is so foundational. But where do we begin?

It's easy to feel overwhelmed by this question. Some may feel the urge to amass a large lump sum and then try to put it all in one product—insurance, investments, liquid assets—to provide all the growth, liquidity, and income they need. Instead, we think you need a more balanced approach. After all, retirement planning isn't magic. As we mention elsewhere, there is no single product that can be all things to all people (or even all things to one person). No approach works unilaterally for everyone. That's why it's important to talk to a financial professional who can help you lay down the basics and take you step-by-step through the process. Not only will you have the assurance you have addressed the areas you need to, but you will also have an ally who can help you break down the process and help keep you from feeling overwhelmed.

Sources of Income

Thinking of all the pieces of your retirement expenses might be intimidating. But, like cleaning out a junk drawer or revisiting that garage remodel, once you have laid everything out, you can begin to sort things into categories.

Once you have a good overall picture of where your expenses will lie, you can start stacking up the resources to cover them.

Social Security

Social Security is a guaranteed, inflation-protected federal insurance program that plays a significant part in most of our retirement plans. From delaying until you've reached full retirement age or beyond to examining spousal benefits, as we discuss elsewhere in this book, there is plenty you can do to try to make the most of this monthly benefit. As with all your retirement income sources, it's important to consider how to make this resource stretch to provide the most bang and buck for your situation.

Pension

Another generally reliable source of retirement income for you might be a pension, if you are one of the lucky people who still has one.

If you don't have a pension, go ahead and skim on to the next section. If you do have a pension, keep on reading.

Because your pension can be such a central piece of your retirement income plan, you will want to put some thought into answering basic questions about it.

How well is your pension funded? Since the heyday of the pension plan, companies and governments have neglected to fund their pension obligations, causing a persistent problem with this otherwise reliable asset. However, research conducted by the Pew Charitable Trusts showed a collective increase in assets exceeding half a trillion dollars in state retirement plans fueled by strong market investment returns in fiscal 2021. Pew's estimates that state retirement systems rose to 80 percent funding for the first time in 2008.[21]

Consider the factors at play, though. Pensions had been underfunded and gained a boost from strong market performance in 2021. What happens to the solvency of those pension funds if the market declines?

It can be worthwhile to keep tabs on your pension's health and know what your options are for withdrawing your pension. If you have already retired and made those decisions, this may be a foregone conclusion. If not, it pays to know what you can expect and what decisions you can make, such as taking spousal options to cover your husband or wife if he or she outlives you.

Also, some companies are incentivizing lump-sum payouts of pensions to reduce the companies' payment liabilities. If that's the case with your employer, talk to your financial

---

[21] pewtrusts.org. September 14, 2021. "The State Pension Funding Gap: Plans Have Stabilized in Wake of Pandemic"
https://www.pewtrusts.org/en/research-and-analysis/issue-briefs/2021/09/the-state-pension-funding-gap-plans-have-stabilized-in-wake-of-pandemic

professional to see if it might be prudent to do something like that, or if it might be better to stick with lifetime payments or other options.

Your 401(k) and IRA

One "modern way" to save for retirement is in a 401(k) or IRA (or their nonprofit or governmental equivalents). These tax-advantaged accounts are, in our opinion, a poor substitute for pensions. However, it can be a mistake not to take full advantage of opportunities to invest in employer-sponsored 401(k)s or IRAs. According to one article, only 32 percent of Americans invest in a 401(k), though 59 percent of employed Americans have access to a 401(k) benefit option.[22]

Also, if you have changed jobs over the years, do the work of tracking down any benefits from your past employers. You might have an IRA here or a 401(k) there; keep track of those so you can pull them together and look at those assets when you're ready to look at establishing sources of retirement income.

Do You Have...

- Life insurance?
- Annuities?
- Long-term care insurance?
- Any passive income sources?
- Stock and bond portfolios?
- Liquid assets? (What's in your bank account?)
- Alternative investments?
- Rental properties?

---

[22] Amin Dabit. personalcapital.com. April 1, 2021. "The Average 401k Balance by Age." https://www.personalcapital.com/blog/retirement-planning/average-401k-balance-age/

If you are going through the work of sitting with a financial professional, it's important to look at your full retirement income picture and pull together *all* your assets, no matter how big or small. From the free insurance policy offered at your bank to the sizable investment in your brother-in-law's modestly successful furniture store, you want to have a good idea of where your money is.

We began working with Patrick and Lisa a few years ago. They are a couple in their mid-sixties who retired with $1,500,000 in investable assets and no debt. Annual Social Security income collectively was $60,000, and expenses were easily covered.

We took Patrick and Lisa through the five pillars of *Bogey-Free Retirement*:

1. **Income** was solid and covered expenses.
2. **Investments** were divided into protection and growth buckets. Withdrawals would come from the protection bucket as needed. The growth bucket was left to grow for five or ten years (or longer). This eliminated sequence of return risk.
3. **Taxes**: They worked with a CPA firm to lower their taxes.
4. **Health care**: They decided to take 1 percent of their investable assets on a yearly basis and fund a hybrid life insurance/LTCI product.
5. **Legacy**: We referred them to a qualified estate planning attorney and they devised a trust-based plan.

Nevertheless, Patrick still worried they did not have enough, even though Lisa assured him they did. This was unchartered territory. He was retired, not drawing a paycheck, and not contributing to his plan. He was drawing down his assets and this worried him. It wasn't until the end of 2022, with the S&P 500 down 19 percent, that he could see the value of market-based investments along with protected accounts. Sure, their market-based investments were down in value, but their protected accounts either remained level or slightly positive.

Patrick and Lisa could now "see" their plan in action and felt a renewed confidence that they would be all right.

Retirement Income Needs

How much income will you need in retirement? How do you determine that? A lot of people work toward a random number, thinking, "If I can just have a million dollars, I'll be comfortable in retirement!" Don't get us wrong; it is possible to save up a lot of money and then retire in the hopes you can keep your monthly expenses lower than some set estimation. But we think this carries a general risk of running out of money. Instead, we work with our clients to find out what their current and projected income needs are and then work from there to see how we might cover any gaps between what they have and what they want.

Goals and Dreams

We like to start with your pie-in-the-sky aspirations. Do you find yourself planning for your vacations more thoroughly than you do your retirement? It's not uncommon for Americans to spend more time planning our vacations than we spend planning our retirement. Maybe it's because planning a vacation is less stressful: Having a week at the beach go awry is, well, a walk on the beach compared to running out of money in retirement. Whatever the case, perhaps it would be better if you thought of your retirement as a vacation in and of itself—no clocking in, no boss, no overtime. If you felt unlimited by financial strain, what would you do?

We had the pleasure of attending the Masters in 2013 and 2015. This was one of our "bucket list" items and we've been trying to get back ever since—if you have extra tickets, give us a call!

What is on your bucket list? Perhaps a long vacation in Paris or Rome? Would it mean mentoring at children's clubs or serving at the local soup kitchen? Or maybe it would mean deepening your ties to those immediately around you—neighbors, friends, and family. Would you be more active in your church? Maybe it would mean more time to take part in the hobbies and activities you love. Have you been considering a second (or even third) act as a small-business owner, turning a hobby or passion into a revenue source?

After that, it's a matter of putting a dollar amount on it. What are the costs of round-the-world travel? One couple we know said their highest priority in retirement was being able to take each of their grandchildren on a cross-country vacation every year. That's a specific goal—one that is reasonably easy to nail down and budget for.

This is your time to gaze into the future and dare to daydream with only one question in mind:

If you could do anything, what would you do?

Current Budget

Compiling a current expense report is one of the trickiest pieces of retirement preparation. Many people assume the expenses of their lives in retirement will be different—lower. After all, there will be no drive to work, no need for a formal wardrobe, and, perhaps most impactful of all, no more saving for retirement!

Yet, we often underestimate our daily spending habits. That's why we typically ask our clients to bring in their bank statements for the past year—they are reflective of your *actual* spending, not just what you think you're spending.

First, we ask clients to develop a balance sheet and net worth statement. We have them look at all sources of income: Social Security, pensions, and investments. Then, we look at liabilities: mortgages and loans, etc. Next, we look at lifestyle: the price of a home, property taxes, hobbies, and travel. We'll know how much they have in fixed income, how much their lifestyle will cost, and how much we might need to supplement their income needs from their investment portfolio.

We can't count the number of times we have sat with a couple, asked them about their spending, and heard them throw out a number that seemed incredibly low. When we ask them where the number came from, they usually say they estimated based on their total bills. Yet our spending is so much more than our mortgage, utilities, cable, phone, car, grocery, or credit card bills.

"What about clothes?" we ask, "Or dining out? What about gifts and coffees and last-minute birthday cards?" That's when the lights come on.

This is why we suggest collecting a year's worth of information. There is usually no such thing as a one-time purchase. Did you buy new furniture? Even if that is a rarity, do you think that will be the last time you *ever* buy furniture?

When we think about budgeting, two very different couples come to mind. The first couple had a scarcity mindset. Their net worth was $5,000,000, but they lived as though they were poor. It may have had something to do with growing up during the Great Depression. No amount of returns ever seemed to satisfy them. If the market declined, they acted as though they would be homeless. They lived in a nice home but had trouble spending and enjoying their money.

The second couple had an abundance mentality. They lived modestly on two Social Security checks. They were debt-free but had very little in investments. However, they were one of the happiest couples I have ever met. They took missionary trips to foreign countries that were sponsored by donations. As they described how they lived, it reminded me of the classic movie, *It's A Wonderful Life.*

One couple had plenty of money; the other had little. The first couple was unhappy; the second radiated joy and lived life abundantly by serving others. Sometimes it's about more than money; it's about the mindset.

Another hefty expense is spending on the kids. Many of the couples we work with are quick to help their adult children, whether it's something like letting them live in the basement, paying for college, babysitting, paying an occasional bill, or contributing to a grandchild's college fund. Research concluded that 22 percent of adults receive some kind of financial support from parents. That segment jumps to almost 30 percent when factoring in the generation we call millennials.[23]

Our clients sometimes protest that what they do for their grown children can stop in retirement. They don't *need* to help. But we get it. Parents like to feel needed. And, while you never want to neglect saving for retirement in favor of taking on financial risks (like your child's student debt), the parents who help their adult children do so in part because it helps them feel fulfilled.

When it comes down to expenses, including (and especially) spending on your family, don't make your initial calculations based on what you *could* whittle your budget down to if you *had* to. Instead, start from where you are. Who wants to live off a bare-bones bank account in retirement?

Other Expenses

Once you have nailed down your current budget and your dreams or goals for retirement, there are a few other outstanding pieces to think about—some expenses many people don't take the time to consider before making and executing a plan. But we're assuming you want to get it right, so let's take a look.

Housing

Do you know where you want to live in retirement? This makes up a substantial piece of your income puzzle—since the typical American household owns a home, and it's generally their largest asset.

---

[23] Kamaron McNair. magnifymoney.com. October 26, 2021. "Nearly 30% of Millenials Still Receive Financial Support From Their Parents" https://www.magnifymoney.com/blog/news/parental-financial-support-survey/

Some people prefer to live right where they are for as long as they can. Others have been waiting for retirement to pull the trigger on an ambitious move, like purchasing a new house, or even downsizing. Whatever your plans and whatever your reasons, there are quite a few things to consider.

Mortgage

Do you still have a mortgage? What may have been a nice tax boon in your working years could turn into a financial burden in your retirement. After all, when you are on a limited income, a mortgage is just one more bill sapping your financial strength. It is something to put some thought into, whether you plan to age in place or are considering moving to your dream home, buying a house out of state, or living in a retirement community.

Upkeep and Taxes

A house without a mortgage still requires annual taxes. While it's tempting to think of this as a once-a-year expense, when you have limited earning potential, your annual tax bill might be something into which you should put a little more forethought.

The costs of homeownership aren't just monetary. When you find yourself dealing with more house than you need, it can drain your time and energy. From keeping clutter at bay to keeping the lawn mower running, upkeep can be extensive and expensive. For some, that's a challenge they heartily accept and can comfortably take on. For others, the idea of yard work or cleaning an area larger than they need feels foolish.

For instance, Peggy discovered after her knee replacement that most of her house was inaccessible to her when she was laid up.

"It felt ridiculous to pay someone else to dust and vacuum a house I was only living in 40 percent of!"

Practicality and Adaptability

Erik and Magda are looking to retire within the next two decades. They just sold their old three-bedroom ranch-style house. Their twins are in high school, and the couple has wanted to "upgrade" for years. Now they live in a gorgeous 1940s three-story house with all the kitchen space they ever wanted, five sprawling bedrooms, and a library and media room for themselves and their children. Within months of moving in, the couple realized a house perfect for their active teens would no longer be perfect for them in five to fifteen years.

"We are paying the mortgage for this house, but we've started saving for the next one," said Magda, "because who wants to climb two flights of stairs to their bedroom when they're seventy-eight?"

Others we know have encountered a similar situation in their personal lives. After a health crisis, one couple found the luxurious tub for two they toiled to install had become a specter of a bad slip and a potential safety risk. It's important to think through what your physical reality could be. We always emphasize to our clients that they should plan for whatever their long-term future might hold, but it's amazing how many people don't give it much thought.

Contracts and Regulations

If you are looking into a cross-country move, be aware of new tax tables or local ordinances in the area where you are looking to move. After all, you don't want to experience sticker-shock when you are looking at downsizing or reducing your bills in retirement.

Along the same lines, if you are moving into a retirement community, be sure to look at the fine print. What happens if you must move into a different situation for long-term care? Will you be penalized? Will you be responsible for replacing your slot in the community? What are all the fees, and what do they cover?

Inflation

As we write this in 2023, America has experienced a wave of inflation following a lengthy period of low inflation. Inflation zoomed to 9.1 percent in June 2022, its highest mark since November 1981.[24]

Core inflation is yet another measurement that excludes goods with prices that tend to be more volatile, such as food and energy costs. Core inflation for a 12-month period ending in December 2022 was 5.7 percent. It so happened energy prices rose 7.3 percent over that timeframe.[25]

However, inflation isn't a one-time bump; it has a cumulative effect. Again, that can impact the price of groceries greater than other goods. Even with relatively low inflation over the past few decades, an item you bought in 1997 for two dollars will cost about $3.70 today.[26] Want to go to a show? A $20 ticket in 1997 would cost $43.01 in 2023.[27]

What if, in retirement, we hit a stretch like the late seventies and early eighties, when annual inflation rates of 10 percent became the norm? It may be wise to consider some extra padding in your retirement income plan to account for any potential increase in inflation in the future.

---

[24] tradingeconomics.com. 2022 Data/2023 Forecast/1914-2021 Historical. "United States Inflation Rate" https://tradingeconomics.com/united-states/inflation-cpi

[25] U.S. Inflation Calculator. "United States Core Inflation Rates (1957-2022)" https://www.usinflationcalculator.com/inflation/united-states-core-inflation-rates/

[26] In2013dollars.com. "$2 in 1997 is worth $3.70 today" https://www.in2013dollars.com/us/inflation/1997?amount=2

[27] In2013dollars.com "Admission to movies, theaters, and concerts priced at $20 in 1997>$40.34 in 2022" https://www.in2013dollars.com/Admission-to-movies,-theaters,-and-concerts/price-inflation

Aging

Also, in the expense category, think about longevity. We all hope to age gracefully. However, it's important to face the prospect of aging with a sense of realism.

The elephant in the room for many families is long-term care. No one wants to admit they will likely need it, but estimates indicate almost 70 percent of us will.[28] Aging is a significant piece of retirement income planning because you'll want to figure out how to set aside money for your care, either at home or away from it. The more comfortable you get with discussing your wishes and plans with your loved ones, the easier planning for the financial side of it can be.

We denote health care and potential long-term care costs in more detail elsewhere in this book, but suffice it to say, nursing home care tends to be very expensive and typically isn't something you get to choose when you will need.

It isn't just the costs of long-term care that pose a concern in living longer. It's also about covering the possible costs of everything else associated with living longer. For instance, if Henry retires from his job as a biochemical engineer at age sixty-five, perhaps he planned to have a very decent income for twenty years, until age eighty-five. But what if he lives until he's ninety-five? That's a whole third—ten years—more of personal income he will need.

Putting It All Together

Whew! So, you have pulled together what you have, and you have a pretty good idea of where you want to be. Now your financial professional and you can go about the work of arranging what assets you *have* to cover what you *need*—and how you might try to cover any gaps.

---

[28] Moll Law Group. 2022. "The Cost of Long-Term Care." https://www.molllawgroup.com/the-cost-of-long-term-care.html

Let's look at the story of the wise and foolish builders in Matthew 7:24-27.[29]

"Therefore everyone who hears these words of mine and puts them into practice is like a wise man who built his house on the rock. The rain came down, the streams rose, and the winds blew and beat against that house; yet it did not fall, because it had its foundation on the rock. But everyone who hears these words of mine and does not put them into practice is like a foolish man who built his house on sand. The rain came down, the streams rose, and the winds blew and beat against that house, and it fell with a great crash."

Just like this Bible story, we encourage our clients to build a solid financial foundation on their way to a *Bogey-Free Retirement*.

Again, you should keep in mind there isn't one single financial vehicle, asset, or source to fill all your needs, and that's okay. One of the challenges of planning for your income in retirement concerns figuring out what products and strategies to use. You can release some of that stress when you accept the fact you will probably need a diverse portfolio—potentially with bonds, stocks, insurance, and other income sources—not just one massive money pile.

One way to help shore up your income gaps is by working with your financial professional and a qualified tax advisor to mitigate your tax exposure. If you have a 401(k) or IRA, a tax advisor in your corner can help you figure out how and when to take distributions from your account in a way that doesn't push you into a higher tax bracket. Or you might learn how to use tax-advantaged bonds more effectively. Effective tax planning isn't necessarily about "adding" to your income. Especially regarding retirement, it's less about what you make than it is about what you keep. Paying a lower tax bill keeps more money in your pocket, which is where you want it when it comes to retirement income.

---

[29] Bible.com. "Matthew 7:24-27." https://www.bible.com/bible/1/MAT.7.24-27.KJV.

Now you can look at ways to cover your remaining retirement goals. Are there products like long-term care insurance specific to a certain kind of expense you anticipate? Is there a particular asset you want to use for your "play" money—money for trips and gifts for the grandkids? Is there any way you can portion off money for those charitable legacy plans?

Once you have analyzed your income wants, needs, and the assets to realistically cover them, you may have a gap. The masterstroke of a competent financial professional will be to help you figure out how you will cover that gap. Will you need to cut out a round of golf a week? Maybe skip the new car? Or will you need to take more substantial action?

One way to cover an income gap is to consider working longer or even part-time before retirement and even after that magical calendar date. This may not be the best "plan" for you; disabilities, work demands, and physical or emotional limitations can hinder the best-laid plans to continue working. However, if it is physically possible for you, this is one considerable way to help your assets last, for more than one reason.

In fact, 46 percent of the Americans responding to a survey report they plan to work part-time after retiring, while 18 percent indicated they planned to work past the age of seventy.[30]

When you're retired, you no longer have an employer paying you a steady check. It is up to you to make sure you have saved and planned for the income you need.

---

[30] Palash Ghosh. Forbes.com. May 6, 2021. "A Third Of Seniors Seek To Work Well Past Retirement Age, Or Won't Retire At All, Poll Finds" https://www.forbes.com/sites/palashghosh/2021/05/06/a-third-of-seniors-seek-to-work-well-past-retirement-age-or-wont-retire-at-all-poll-finds/?sh=1d2ece836b95

CHAPTER 5

Social Security

Social Security is often the foundation of retirement income. Backed by the strength of the U.S. Treasury, it provides perhaps the most dependable paycheck you will have in retirement.

From the time you collect your first paycheck from the job that made you a bonafide taxpayer, you are paying into the grand old Social Security system. What grew and developed out of the pressures of the Great Depression has become one of the most popular government programs in the country, and if you pay in for the equivalent of ten years or more, you, too, can benefit from the Social Security program.

Now, before we get into the nitty-gritty of Social Security, we'd like to address a current concern: Will Social Security still be there for you when you reach retirement age?

The Future of Social Security

This question is ever-present as headlines trumpet an underfunded Social Security program, alongside the sea of baby boomers retiring in droves and the comparatively smaller pool of younger people who are funding the system.

The Social Security Administration itself acknowledges this concern as each Social Security statement now contains a link to its website (ssa.gov) and a page entitled, "Will Social Security Be There For Me?"

Just a reminder—as if you needed one—that nothing in life is guaranteed. Additionally, depending on who you're listening to, Social Security funds may run low before 2034 thanks to the financial instability and government spending that accompanied the 2020 COVID-19 pandemic.

Before you get too discouraged, though, here are a few thoughts to keep you going:

- Even if the program is only paying 78 cents on the dollar for scheduled benefits, 78 percent is notably not zero.
- The Social Security Administration has made changes in the distant and near past to protect the fund's solvency, including increasing retirement ages and striking certain filing strategies.
- There are many changes Congress could make, and lawmakers routinely discuss how to fix the system, such as further increasing full retirement age and eligibility.
- One thing no one is seriously discussing? Reneging on current obligations to retirees or the soon-to-retire.

Take heart. The real answer to the question, "Will Social Security be there for me?" is still yes.

This question is important to consider when you look at how much we, as a nation, rely on this program. Did you know Social Security benefits replace about 40 percent of a person's original income when they retire?[31]

If you ask us, that's a pretty significant piece of your retirement income puzzle.

Another caveat? You may not realize this, but no one can legally "advise" you about your Social Security benefits.

"But, Mark and Jordan," you may be thinking, "isn't that part of what you do? And what about that nice gentleman at the

---

[31] ssa.gov. "Alternate Measure of Replacement Rates for Social Security Benefits and Retirement Income" https://www.ssa.gov/policy/docs/ssb/v68n2/v68n2p1.html.

Social Security Administration office I spoke with on the phone?"

Don't get us wrong; Social Security Administration employees know their stuff. They are trained to understand policies and programs, and they are usually pretty quick to tell you what you can and cannot do. But the government specifically stipulates, because Social Security is a benefit you alone have paid into and earned, your Social Security decisions, too, are yours alone.

When it comes to financial professionals, we can't push you in any direction, but—and there's a big but here—working with a well-informed financial professional is still incredibly handy for your Social Security decisions. Why? Because someone who's worth his or her salt will know what withdrawal strategies might pertain to your specific situation and will ask questions that can help you determine what you are looking for when it comes to your Social Security.

For instance, some people want the highest possible monthly benefit. Others want to start their benefits early, not always because of financial need. We heard about one man who called in to start his Social Security payments the day he qualified, just because he liked to think of it as the government paying back a debt it owed him, and he enjoyed the feeling of receiving a check from Uncle Sam.

Whatever your reasons, questions, or feelings regarding Social Security, the decision is yours alone; but working with a financial professional can help you put your options in perspective by showing you—both with industry knowledge and with proprietary software or planning processes—where your benefits fit into your overall strategy for retirement income.

One reason the federal government doesn't allow for "advice" related to Social Security, we suspect, is so no one can profit from giving you advice related to your Social Security benefit—or from providing any clarifications. Again, this is a sign of a good financial professional. Those who are passionate about their work will be knowledgeable about what benefit strategies might be to your advantage and will happily share those possible options with you.

Full Retirement Age

When it comes to Social Security, it seems like many people only think so far as "yes." They don't take the time to understand the various options available. Instead, because it is common knowledge you can begin your benefits at age sixty-two, that's what many of us do. While more people are opting to delay taking benefits, age sixty-two is still firmly the most popular age to start.[32]

What many people fail to understand is, by starting benefits early, they may be leaving a lot of money on the table. You see, the Social Security Administration bases your monthly benefit on two factors: your earnings history and your full retirement age (FRA).

From your earnings history, they pull the thirty-five years you made the most money and use a mathematical indexing formula to figure out a monthly average from those years. If you paid into the system for less than thirty-five years, then every year you didn't pay in will be counted as a zero.

Once they have calculated what your monthly earning would be at FRA, the government then calculates what to put on your check based on how close you are to FRA. FRA was originally set at sixty-five, but, as the population aged and lifespans lengthened, the government shifted FRA later and later, based on an individual's year of birth. Check out the following chart to see when you will reach FRA.[33]

---

[32] Chris Kissell. moneytalknews.com. January 20, 2021. "This Is When the Most People Start Taking Social Security."
https://www.moneytalksnews.com/the-most-popular-age-for-claiming-social-security/

[33] Social Security Administration. "Full Retirement Age."
https://www.ssa.gov/planners/retire/retirechart.html

Age to Receive Full Social Security Benefits*

(Called "full retirement age" [FRA] or "normal retirement age.")

Year of Birth*	FRA
1937 or earlier	65
1938	65 and 2 months
1939	65 and 4 months
1940	65 and 6 months
1941	65 and 8 months
1942	65 and 10 months
1943-1954	66
1955	66 and 2 months
1956	66 and 4 months
1957	66 and 6 months
1958	66 and 8 months
1959	66 and 10 months
1960 and later	67

If you were born on Jan. 1 of any year, you should refer to the previous year. (If you were born on the 1st of the month, we figure your benefit [and your full retirement age] as if your birthday was in the previous month.)

When you reach FRA, you are eligible to receive 100 percent of whatever the Social Security Administration says is your full monthly benefit.

Starting at age sixty-two, for every year before FRA you claim benefits, your monthly check is reduced by 5 percent or more. Conversely, for every year you delay taking benefits past FRA, your monthly benefit increases by 8 percent (until age seventy—after that, there is no monetary advantage to delaying Social Security benefits). While your circumstances and needs may vary, a lot of financial professionals still urge people to at least consider delaying until they reach age seventy.

Why wait?[34]

Taking benefits early could affect your monthly check by _____.								
62	63	64	65	FRA 66	67	68	69	70
-25%	-20%	-13.3%	-6.7%	0	+8%	+16%	+24%	+32%

My Social Security

If you are over age thirty, you have probably received a notice from the Social Security Administration telling you to activate something called "My Social Security." This is a handy way to learn more about your particular benefit options, to keep track of what your earnings record looks like, and to calculate the benefits you have accrued over the years.

Essentially, My Social Security is an online account you can activate to see what your personal Social Security picture looks like, which you can do at www.ssa.gov/myaccount. This can be extremely helpful when it comes to planning for income in retirement and figuring out the difference between your anticipated income versus anticipated expenses.

My Social Security is also helpful because it's a great way to see if there is a problem. For instance, we have heard of one

---

[34] Social Security Administration. April 2021. "Can You Take Your Benefits Before Full Retirement Age?"
https://www.ssa.gov/planners/retire/applying2.html

woman who, through diligently checking her tax records against her Social Security profile, discovered her Social Security check was shortchanging her, based on her earnings history. After taking the discrepancy to the Social Security Administration, they sent her what they owed her in makeup benefits.

COLA

Social Security is a largely guaranteed piece of the retirement puzzle: If you get a statement that reads you should expect $1,000 a month, you can be sure you will receive $1,000 a month. But there is one variable detail, and that is something called the cost-of-living adjustment, or COLA.

The COLA is an increase in your monthly check meant to address inflation in everyday life. After all, your expenses will likely continue to experience inflation in retirement, but you will no longer have the opportunity for raises, bonuses, or promotions you had when you were working. Instead, Social Security receives an annual cost-of-living increase tied to the Department of Labor's Consumer Price Index for Urban Wage Earners and Clerical Workers, or CPI-W. If the CPI-W measurement shows inflation rose a certain amount for regular goods and services, then Social Security recipients will see that reflected in their COLA.

COLA adjustments have climbed as high as 14.3 percent (1980) and in 2022 reached 8.7 percent, the largest increase in more than forty years. But in a no or low inflation environment, such as in 2009, 2010, and 2015, Social Security recipients will not receive an adjustment.[35] Some view the COLA as a perk, bump, or bonus, but, in reality, it works more like this: Your mom sends you to the store with $2.50 for a gallon of milk. Milk costs exactly $2.50. The next week, you go back with that same amount, but it is now $2.52 for a gallon, so you go back to Mom,

---

[35] ssa.gov. "Cost-Of-Living Adjustments." ssa.gov/oact/cola/colaseries.html.

and she gives you 2 cents. You aren't bringing home more milk—it just costs more money.

So the COLA is less about "making more money" and more about keeping seniors' purchasing power from eroding when inflation is a big factor, such as in 1975, when it was 8 percent![36] Still, don't let that detract from your enthusiasm about COLAs; after all, what if Mom's solution was: "Here's the same $2.50; try to find pennies from somewhere else to get that milk!"?

Spousal Benefits

We've talked about FRA, but another big Social Security decision involves spousal benefits.

If you or your spouse has a long stretch of zeros in your earnings history—perhaps if one of you stayed home for years, caring for children or sick relatives—you may want to consider filing for spousal benefits instead of filing on your own earnings history. A spousal benefit can be up to 50 percent of the primary wage earner's benefit at full retirement age.

To begin drawing a spousal benefit, you must be at least sixty-two years old, and the primary wage earner must have already filed for his or her benefit. While there are penalties for taking spousal benefits early (you could lose up to 67.5 percent of your check for filing at age sixty-two), you cannot earn credits for delaying past full retirement age.[37]

As we stated, the spousal benefit can be a big deal for those who don't have a very long pay history, but it's important to weigh your own earned benefits against the option of withdrawing based on a fraction of your spouse's benefits.

To look at how this could play out, let's use a hypothetical couple: Mary Jane, who is sixty, and Peter, who is sixty-two.

---

[36] Social Security Administration. "Cost-Of-Living Adjustment (COLA) Information for 2022." https://www.ssa.gov/cola/

[37] Social Security Administration. "Retirement Planner: Benefits For You As A Spouse." https://www.ssa.gov/planners/retire/applying6.html

Let's say Peter's benefit at FRA, in his case sixty-six, would be $1,600. If Peter begins his benefits right now, four years before FRA, his monthly check will be $1,200. If Mary Jane begins taking spousal benefits in two years at the earliest date possible, her monthly benefits will be reduced by 67.5 percent, to $520 per month (remember, at FRA, the most she can qualify for is half of Peter's FRA benefit).

What if Peter and Mary Jane both wait until FRA? At sixty-six, Peter begins taking his full benefit of $1,600 a month. Two years later, when she reaches age sixty-six, Mary Jane will qualify for $800 a month. By waiting until FRA, the couple's monthly benefit goes from $1,720 to $2,400.

What if Peter delays until age seventy to get his maximum possible benefit? For each year past FRA he delays, his monthly benefits increase by 8 percent. This means, at seventy, he could file for a monthly benefit of $2,048. However, delayed retirement credits do not affect spousal benefits, so as soon as Peter files at seventy, Mary Jane would also file (at age sixty-eight) for her maximum benefit of $800, so their highest possible combined monthly check is $2,815.[38]

When it comes to your Social Security benefits, you obviously will want to consider whether a monthly check based on a fraction of your spouse's earnings will be comparable to or larger than your own earnings history.

Divorced Spouses

There are a few considerations for those of us who have gone through a divorce. If you 1) were married for ten years or more *and* 2) have since been divorced for at least two years *and* 3) are unmarried *and* 4) your ex-spouse qualifies to begin Social Security, you qualify for a spousal benefit based on your ex-husband or ex-wife's earnings history at FRA. A divorced

---

[38] Office of the Chief Actuary. Social Security Administration. "Social Security Benefits: Benefits for Spouses."
https://www.ssa.gov/OACT/quickcalc/spouse.html#calculator

spousal benefit is different from the married spousal benefit in one way: You don't have to wait for your ex-spouse to file before you can file yourself.[39]

For instance, Charles and Moira were married for fifteen years before their divorce, when he was thirty-six and she was forty. Moira has been remarried for twenty years, and, although Charles briefly remarried, his second marriage ended after a few years. Charles' benefits are largely calculated based on his many years of volunteering in schools, meaning his personal monthly benefit is close to zero.

Although Moira has deferred her retirement, opting to delay benefits until she is seventy, Charles can begin taking benefits calculated from Moira's work history at FRA as early as sixty-two. However, he will also have the option of waiting until FRA to collect the maximum, or 50 percent of Moira's earned monthly benefit at her FRA.

Widowed Spouses

If your marriage ended with the death of your spouse, you might claim a benefit for your spouse's earned income as his or her widow/widower, called a survivor's benefit. Unlike a spousal benefit or divorced benefits, if your husband or wife dies, you can claim his or her full benefit. Also, unlike spousal benefits, if you need to, you can begin taking income when you turn sixty. However, as with other benefit options, your monthly check will be permanently reduced for withdrawing benefits before FRA.

If your spouse began taking benefits before they died, you can't delay withdrawing your survivor's benefits to get delayed credits. The Social Security Administration maintains you can

---

[39] Social Security Administration. "Retirement Planner: If You Are Divorced." https://www.ssa.gov/planners/retire/divspouse.html

only get as much from a survivor's benefit as your deceased spouse might have received, had they lived.[40]

Taxes, Taxes, Taxes

With Social Security, as with everything, it is important to consider taxes. It may be surprising, but your Social Security benefits are not tax-free. Despite having been taxed to accrue those benefits in the first place, you may have to pay Uncle Sam income taxes on up to 85 percent of your Social Security.

The Social Security Administration figures these taxes using what they call "the provisional income formula." Your provisional income formula differs from the adjusted gross income you use for your regular income taxes. Instead, to find out how much of your Social Security benefit is taxable, the Social Security Administration calculates it this way:

Provisional Income = Adjusted Gross Income + Nontaxable Interest + ½ of Social Security

See that piece about nontaxable interest? That generally means interest from government bonds and notes. It surprises many people that, although you may not pay taxes on those assets, their income will count against you when it comes to Social Security taxation.

Once you have figured out your provisional income (also called "combined income"), you can use the following chart to figure out your Social Security taxes.[41]

---

[40] Social Security Administration. "Social Security Benefit Amounts For The Surviving Spouse By Year Of Birth." https://www.ssa.gov/planners/survivors/survivorchartred.html

[41] Social Security Administration. "Benefits Planner: Income Taxes and Your Social Security Benefits." https://www.ssa.gov/planners/taxes.html

Taxes on Social Security

Provisional Income = Adjusted Gross Income + Nontaxable Interest + ½ of Social Security		
If you are ___ and your provisional income is___, then...		Uncle Sam will tax ___ of your Social Security
Single	Married, filing jointly	
Less than $25,000	Less than $32,000	0%
$25,000 to $34,000	$32,000 to $44,000	Up to 50%
More than $34,000	More than $44,000	Up to 85%

This is one more reason it may benefit you to work with financial and tax professionals. They can look at your entire financial picture to make your overall retirement plan as tax-efficient as possible—including your Social Security benefit.

Working and Social Security: The Earnings Test

If you haven't reached FRA, but you started your Social Security benefits and are still working, things get a little hairy.

Because you have started Social Security payments, the Social Security Administration will pay out your benefits (at that reduced rate, of course, because you haven't reached your FRA). Yet, because you are working, the organization must also withhold from your check to add to your benefits, which you are already collecting. See how this complicates matters?

To address the situation, the government has what is called the earnings test. For 2023, you can earn up to $21,240 without it affecting your Social Security check if you're younger than full retirement age. But, for every $2 you earn past that amount, the Social Security Administration will withhold $1. The earnings test loosens in the year of your FRA; if you are reaching FRA in 2023, you can earn up to $56,520 before you run into the earnings test, and the government only withholds $1 for every $3 past that amount.

The month you reach FRA, you are no longer subject to any earnings withholding. For instance, if you are still working and will turn sixty-six on December 28, 2023, you would only have to worry about the earnings test until December, and then you can ignore it entirely. Keep in mind, the money the government withholds from your Social Security benefits while you are working before FRA will be tacked back onto your benefits check after FRA.[42]

---

[42] Social Security Administration. "Exempt Amounts Under the Earnings Test." https://www.ssa.gov/oact/cola/rtea.html

CHAPTER 6

401(k)s & IRAs

Have you heard? Today's retirement is not your parents' retirement. You see, back in the day, it was pretty common to work for one company for the vast majority of your career and then retire with a gold watch and a pension.

The gold watch was a symbol of the quality time you had put in at that company, but the pension was more than a symbol. Instead, it was a guarantee—as solid as your employer—that they would repay your hard work with a certain amount of income in your old age. Did you see the caveat there? Your pension's guarantee was *as solid as your employer*. The problem was, what if your employer went under?

Companies that failed couldn't pay their retired employees' pensions, leading to financial challenges for many. Beginning in 1974 with Congress' passage of the Employee Retirement Income Security Act, federal legislation and regulations aimed at protecting retirees were everywhere. One piece of legislation included a relatively obscure section of the Internal Revenue Code, added in 1978: Section 401(k), to be specific.

IRC Section 401, Subsection k, created tax advantages for employer-sponsored financial products, even if the main contributor was the employee him or herself. Over the years, more employers took note, beginning an age of transition away from pensions and toward 401(k) plans. A 401(k) is a retirement account with certain tax benefits and restrictions on the investments or other financial products inside of it.

Essentially, 401(k)s and their individual retirement account (IRA) counterparts are "wrappers" that provide tax benefits around assets; typically, the assets that compose IRAs and 401(k)s are mutual funds, stock and bond mixes, and money market accounts. However, IRA and 401(k) contents are becoming more diverse these days, with some companies offering different kinds of annuity options within their plans.

Where pensions are defined-*benefit* plans, 401(k)s and IRAs are defined-*contribution* plans. The one-word change outlines the basic difference. Pensions spell out what you can expect to receive from the plan but not necessarily how much money it will take to fund those benefits. With 401(k)s, an employer sets a standard for how much they will contribute (if any), and you can be certain of what you are contributing. Still, there is no outline for what you can expect to receive in return for those contributions.

Modern employment looks very different. A 2022 survey by the Bureau of Labor Statistics determined U.S. workers stayed with their employers a median of 4.1 years. Workers ages fifty-five to sixty-four had a little more staying power and were most likely to stay with their employer for about ten years.[43] Participation in 401(k) plans has steadily risen this century, totaling $7,300,000,000,000 ($7.3 trillion) in assets in 2021 compared to $3,100,000,000,000 ($3.1 trillion) in 2011. About 60 million active participants engaged in 401(k) plans in 2020.[44]

Those statistics make it clear that 401(k) plans have replaced pensions at many companies and, for that matter, a gold watch.

Let's take a look at two couples: Joe and Sandra are retired educators whose pension income is $160,000 annually. They also draw two Social Security checks, so their total income is $220,000. They have substantial qualified plans, so their

---

[43] Bureau of Labor Statistics. September 22, 2020. "Employee Tenure Summary." https://www.bls.gov/news.release/tenure.nr0.htm
[44] Investment Company Institute. October 11, 2021. "Frequently Asked Questions About 401(k) Plan Research" https://www.ici.org/faqs/faq/401k/faqs_401k#:~:text=

income will go up even more at age seventy-three when they begin to take RMDs. They want the majority of their investable assets in an aggressive growth portfolio since they find it hard to spend all of their income. Assuming they live into their eighties or nineties, the aggressive portfolio could provide a substantial inheritance or be added resources for long-term care needs.

The second couple, Keith and Janice, are retired from the automotive industry. They do not draw a pension. Instead, they draw two Social Security checks totaling $60,000 annually. They are both sixty years of age. Their home is valued at $600,000. They carry a mortgage at a low rate and do not want to pay it off. Expenses run around $60,000 annually. Any additional income must come from their investment portfolio. Careful consideration must be placed on a proper mix of protection and growth in their portfolio.

If there is anything to learn from this common shift away from pensions, it's that you must look out for yourself. Whether you have worked for a company for two years or twenty, you are still the one who has to look out for your own best interests. That holds doubly true when it comes to preparing for retirement. If you are one of the lucky ones who still has a pension, good for you. But for the rest of us, it is likely a 401(k)—or possibly one of its nonprofit- or government-sector counterparts, a 403(b) or 457 plan—is one of your biggest assets for retirement.

Some employers offer incentives to contribute to their company plans, like a company match. On that subject, we have one thing to say: *Do it!* Nothing in life is free, as they say, but a company match on your retirement funds is about as close to free money as it gets. If you can make the minimum to qualify for your company's match at all, go for it.

Now, it's likely, during our working years, we mostly "set and forget" our 401(k) funding. Because it is tax-advantaged, your employer is taking money from your paycheck—before taxes—and putting it into your plan for you. Maybe you got to pick a selection of investments, or maybe your company only offers one choice of investment in your 401(k). Either way, while you are gainfully employed, your most impactful decision may just be the decision to continue funding your plan in the first place. But when you are ready to retire or move jobs, you have choices to make requiring a little more thought and care.

When you are ready to part ways with your job, you have a few options:
- Leave the money where it is.
- Take the cash (and pay income taxes and perhaps a 10 percent additional federal tax if you are younger than age fifty-nine and a half).
- Transfer the money to another employer plan (if the new plan allows).
- Transfer the money to an IRA.

Now, these are just general options. You will have to decide, hopefully with the help of a financial professional, what's right for you. For instance, 401(k)s are typically pretty closely tied to the companies offering them, so when changing jobs, it may not always be possible to transfer a 401(k) to another 401(k). Leaving the money where it is may also be out of the question—some companies have direct cash payout or rollover policies once someone is no longer employed.

Also, remember what we mentioned earlier about how we change jobs more often these days? That means you likely have a 401(k) with your current company, but you may also have a string of retirement accounts trailing you from other jobs.

When it comes to your retirement income, it's important to be able to pull together *all* your assets, so you can examine what you have and where, and then decide what you will do with it.

Tax-Qualified, Tax-Preferred, Tax-Deferred … Still TAXED

Financial media often cite IRAs and 401(k)s for their tax benefits. After all, with traditional plans, you put your money in, pre-tax, and it hopefully grows for years, even decades, untaxed. That's why these accounts are called "tax-qualified" or "tax-deferred" assets. They aren't *tax-free!* Rarely does Uncle Sam allow business to continue without receiving his piece of the pie, and your retirement assets are no different. If you didn't pay taxes on the front end, you will pay taxes on the money you withdraw from these accounts in retirement. Don't get us wrong: This isn't an inherently good or bad thing; it's just the way it is. It's important to understand, though, for the sake of planning ahead.

In retirement, many people assume they will be in a lower tax bracket. Are you planning to pare down your lifestyle in retirement? Perhaps you are, and perhaps you will have substantially less income in retirement. But many of our clients tell us they want to live life more or less the same as they always have. The money they would previously have spent on business attire or gas for their commute they now want to spend on hobbies and grandchildren. That's all fine, and for many of them, it is doable, but does it put them in a lower tax bracket? Probably not.

Keep in mind, IRAs, 401(k)s, and their alternatives have a few limitations because of their special tax status. For one thing, the IRS sets limits on your contributions to these retirement accounts. If you are contributing to a 401(k) or an equivalent nonprofit or government plan, your annual contribution limit is $22,500 (as of 2023). If you are fifty or older, the IRS allows additional contributions—called "catch-up contributions"—of up to $7,500 on top of the regular limit of $22,500. For an IRA, the limit is $6,500, with a catch-up limit of an additional $1,000.[45]

Because their tax advantages come from their intended use as retirement income, withdrawing funds from these accounts before you turn fifty-nine-and-one-half can carry stiff

---

[45] IRS.gov. December 8, 2022. "401(k) limit increases to $22,500 for 2023, IRA limit rises to $6,500" https://www.irs.gov/newsroom/401k-limit-increases-to-22500-for-2023-ira-limit-rises-to-6500

penalties. In addition to fees your investment management company might charge, you will have to pay income tax *and* a 10 percent federal tax penalty, with few exceptions.

The fifty-nine-and-one-half rule for retirement accounts is incredibly important to remember, especially when you're young. Younger workers are often tempted to cash out an IRA from a previous employer and then are surprised to find their checks missing 20 percent of the account value to income taxes, penalty taxes, and account fees.

Many millennials we see in our practice say, while they may be socking money away in their workplace retirement plan, it is often the *only* place they are saving. This could be problematic later because of the fifty-nine-and-one-half rule; what if you have an emergency? It is important to fund your retirement, but you need to have some liquid assets handy as emergency funds. This can help you avoid breaking into your retirement accounts and incurring taxes and penalties because of the fifty-nine-and-one-half rule.

RMDs

Remember how we talked about the 401(k) or IRA being a "tax wrapper" for your funds? Well, eventually, Uncle Sam will want a bite of that candy bar. So, when you turn seventy-three, the government requires you withdraw a portion of your account, which the IRS calculates based on the size of your account and your estimated lifespan. This required minimum distribution, or RMD, is the government's insurance it will collect some taxes, at some point, from your earnings. Because you didn't pay taxes on the front end, you will now pay income taxes on whatever you withdraw, including your RMDs.

Let me reiterate something I pointed out in the Longevity chapter. Beginning at age seventy-three, you are required to withdraw a certain minimum amount every year from your 401(k) or IRA, or else you will face a tax penalty on any RMD monies you should have withdrawn but didn't—and that's on top of income tax. The SECURE Act 2.0 reduced the penalty to 25 percent (from 50 percent). Timely corrections can also reduce the penalty to 10 percent.[46]

Even after you begin RMDs, you can still also continue contributing to your 401(k) or IRAs if you are still employed, which can affect the whole discussion on RMDs and possible tax considerations. The SECURE Act 2.0 raised the RMD age to seventy-three from seventy-two. In addition, the latest legislation stipulates the RMD age will increase to seventy-five for those turning seventy-four after December 31, 2032.[47]

If you don't need income from your retirement accounts, RMDs can seem like more of a tax burden than an income boon. While some people prefer to reinvest their RMDs, this comes with the possibility of additional taxation: You'll pay income taxes on your RMDs and then potential income or capital gains taxes on the growth of your investments. If you are legacy-minded, there are other ways to use RMDs, many of which have tax benefits.

SECURE Act 2.0 provisions

In addition to changes imposed for RMD ages, Secure Act 2.0 also expanded access to retirement savings using different methods. Provisions in the legislation go into effect at different times, ranging from 2023-25.[48]

- Beginning January 2, 2024, plan participants can access up to $1,000 (once a year) from retirement savings for emergency personal or family expenses without paying a 10 percent early withdrawal penalty.
- Beginning January 2, 2024, employees can establish a Roth emergency savings account within their 401(k) plan of up to $2,500 per participant.

---

[46] Jim Probasco. Investopedia.com. January 6, 2023. "SECURE 2.0 Act of 2022." https://www.investopedia.com/secure-2-0-definition-5225115
[47] Ibid.
[48] Betterment.com. January 12, 2023. "SECURE Act 2.0: Signed into Law." https://www.betterment.com/work/resources/secure-act-2.

- Beginning January 2, 2024, domestic abuse survivors can withdraw the lesser of $10,000 or 50 percent of their retirement account without penalty.
- Beginning January 1, 2023, victims of a qualified, federally declared disaster can withdraw up to $22,000 from their retirement account without penalty.[49]

Permanent Life Insurance

One way to turn those pesky RMDs into a legacy is through permanent life insurance. Assuming you need the death benefit coverage and can qualify for it medically, if properly structured, these products can pass on a sizeable death benefit to your beneficiaries, tax-free, as part of your general legacy plan.

Hank and Millie retired to Tennessee after working hard their entire lives—he in the airline industry and she in real estate. They enjoyed gourmet cooking, ballroom dancing, Caribbean cruises, and rarely missed a performance at the Cumberland County Playhouse. When Hank passed away, she was not at a loss about where things stood financially because as the Chief Financial Officer, CFO, of their family's financials, she was well prepared for the future.

Nevertheless, she still had questions. In a strategy meeting, she asked, "Is there anything else I should do?" We discussed the possibility of permanent life insurance. Her portfolio consisted of stocks, bonds, annuities, cash, and real estate. She decided to take 1 percent of her total net worth and purchase a large permanent life insurance policy. She was already in her seventies, but healthy. When she passed away five years later, she left her sizeable estate to her two daughters—including a substantial amount of tax-free money from the permanent life insurance policy. The daughters once told me they were blown away by their mother's remarkable business acumen.

---

[49] Charlie Pastor. Motley Fool. February 16, 2023. "Law Opens New Doors for Penalty-Free Retirement Account Distributions." Fool.com/the-ascent/buying-stocks/articles/law-opens-new-doors-for-penalty-free-retirement-account-distributions

ILIT

Another way to use RMDs toward your legacy is to work with an estate planning attorney to create an irrevocable life insurance trust (ILIT). This is basically a permanent life insurance policy placed within a trust. Because the trust is irrevocable, you would relinquish control of it, but, unlike with just a permanent life insurance policy, your death benefit won't count toward your taxable estate.

Annuities

Because annuities can be tax-deferred, using all or a portion of your RMDs to fund an annuity contract can be one way to further delay taxation while guaranteeing your income payments (either to you or your loved ones) later. (Assuming you don't need the RMD income during your retirement.)

Qualified Charitable Distributions

If you are charity-minded, you may use your RMDs toward a charitable organization instead of using them for income. You must do this directly from your retirement account (you can't take the RMD check and *then* pay the charity) for your withdrawals to be qualified charitable distributions (QCDs), but this is one way of realizing some of the benefits of a charitable legacy during your own lifetime. You will not need to pay taxes on your QCDs, and they won't count toward your annual charitable tax deduction limit, plus you'll be able to see how the organization you are supporting uses your donations. You should consult a financial professional on how to correctly make a QCD, particularly since the SECURE Act has implemented a few regulations on this point.[50]

---

[50] Bob Carlson. Forbes. January 28, 2020. "More Questions And Answers About The SECURE Act."
https://www.forbes.com/sites/bobcarlson/2020/01/28/more-questions-and-answers-about-the-secure-act/#113d49564869

Roth IRA

Since the Taxpayer Relief Act of 1997, there has been a different kind of retirement account, or "tax wrapper," available to the public: the Roth. Roth IRAs and Roth 401(k)s each differ from their traditional counterparts in one big way: You pay your taxes on the front end. This means, once your post-tax money is in the Roth account, as long as you follow the rules and limitations of that account, your distributions are truly tax-free. You won't pay income tax when you take withdrawals, so, in turn, you don't have to worry about RMDs. However, Roth accounts have the same limitations as traditional 401(k)s and IRAs when it comes to withdrawing money before age fifty-nine-and-one-half, with the added stipulation that the account must have been open for at least five years in order for the account holder to make withdrawals.

Taking Charge

As mentioned earlier, the 401(k) and IRA have largely replaced pensions, but they aren't an equal trade.

Pensions are employer-funded; the money feeding into them is money that wouldn't ever show up on your pay stub. Because 401(k)s are self-funded, you must actively and consciously save. This distinction has made a difference when it comes to funding retirement. Fidelity Investments published a story detailing that the average 401(k) balance for a person age fifty-five to sixty-four is $189,800, but the median likely tells the full story. The median 401(k) balance for a person age fifty-five to sixty-four is $56,450. Those figures reflect Fidelity accounts from the third quarter of 2022.[51]

There can be many reasons why people underfund their retirement plans, like being overwhelmed by investment

---

[51] Arielle O'Shea. Nerd Wallet. December 22, 2022. "The Average 401(k) Balance by Age." https://www.nerdwallet.com/article/investing/the-average-401k-balance-by-age

choices or taking withdrawals from IRAs when they leave an employer. Still, the reason at the top of the list is this: People simply aren't participating to begin with.

So, whether you use a 401(k) with an employer or an IRA alternative with a private company, separate from your workplace, the most important retirement savings decision you can make is to sock away your money somewhere in the first place.

CHAPTER 7

Annuities

It's April. Springtime is here. Dogwoods are in bloom. Let's imagine you're a professional golfer playing on the PGA Tour. And you're not at just any tournament, you're playing the Masters in Augusta, Georgia.

It's 2007 and Zach Johnson is playing in his third Masters tournament. Against the likes of Tiger Woods and Phil Mickelson, he is certainly not the favorite to win. However, Zach Johnson won the 2007 Masters with a four-round score of 1-over par, tied for the highest winning score ever. Cool temperatures and gusty winds contributed to the high scores.

Zach, not considered a long hitter on the PGA Tour, made a decision before the tournament to lay up on every par-five because of the extreme weather conditions. Many questioned his strategy, thinking the long hitters would eventually overtake him because he was too cautious. Zach played the par fives better than anyone in the field that week with eleven birdies and no bogeys. Playing it safe won't win every PGA event, but in retirement, it's almost universal that safety should be part of the plan.

Of all the financial products we work with, it seems people find none more mysterious than annuities. Even some of those who recognize the word "annuity" have a limited understanding of just how they work. Therefore, in the interest of demystifying annuities, let's tee it up and talk about them.

An annuity is a contract between you and an insurance company that can provide a unique combination of insurance, investment, and income features. Annuities may complement other retirement plans and, depending on what type you select, they may also provide guaranteed lifetime income, tax-deferred growth, guaranteed yield, downside protection, index-linked gains, flexible withdrawals, and legacy protection for your beneficiaries.

In general, insurance is a financial hedge against risk. Automobile insurance provides protection against the risk of injury in an accident. Homeowner insurance provides protection against fire, flood, natural disaster, and personal injury. An annuity can provide financial protection by providing a "safety-first" stream of income that could last the remainder of one's life. Let's break down three types of annuities we use in our practice.

Multi-Year Guaranteed Annuity (MYGA)

If you're looking for safety from market volatility, a MYGA could be right for you. A MYGA is a contract with an insurance company whereby you pay a premium in exchange for a guaranteed rate for a specified time period. The time periods can range from two years to ten years. Keep in mind, these types of annuities have surrender charge schedules (early withdrawal penalty) that go along with the terms of two years to ten years. Guarantees are backed by the claims-paying ability of the issuing company.

Chris and Elaine owned a sporting goods store and sold it prior to retirement. Most of their money was tied up in the store until it was sold, so they had a large amount of cash to invest. Since income was their first priority, we invested a portion of their assets in dividend-paying stocks and a portion in MYGAs. The MYGAs were emphasized because of the guaranteed interest rate, resulting in a guaranteed stream of income.

There are several reasons why you might consider a MYGA. Since a MYGA offers a guaranteed interest rate for the entire contracted term, it's considered a less risky investment than stocks or bonds. MYGAs could be used as a supplement to your Social Security benefits or your qualified retirement plans. They can be a predictable source of income during retirement. The interest earned with a MYGA is tax-deferred, meaning you won't owe taxes on growth until you take a distribution. You can purchase a MYGA using funds from qualified plans, non-qualified accounts, or bank accounts. With a qualified account type annuity, you pay income tax on principal and interest when making withdrawals. With non-qualified annuities, only the interest is taxable. The ability to take partial withdrawals without a penalty can be an attractive feature.

Multi-year guaranteed annuities are often mentioned in the same breath as a bank certificate of deposit or CD. With a CD, you deposit your money for a specific period of time. Once the CD reaches the maturity date, you have the option to renew it (at the current interest rate) or withdraw your initial deposit, along with the interest earned. You may also be able to renew a MYGA at the end of your contract. If you do, the interest rate may vary from the interest rate at the beginning of the term.

Much like a CD, you would be offered whatever the current rate is at the time of renewal, which could be higher or lower than what you had been earning. If you choose not to renew your MYGA with a new contract, you could instead withdraw the principal and interest. Your annuity company may allow a penalty-free window to do so, in which you wouldn't face surrender charges. Within that window, you could also transfer the money to another non-qualified annuity using a 1035 exchange or an IRA-to-IRA transfer for a qualified annuity without triggering a tax penalty.

Fixed Index Annuities (FIA)
A fixed index annuity is a contract with an insurance company that earns interest based on changes in a market index. FIAs are long-term insurance products with guarantees backed by the claims-paying ability of the issuing company. Time periods can range from five to fifteen years. These types of annuities

have surrender charge schedules (early withdrawal penalty) that go along with the terms of five to fifteen years. Returns are based on the performance of an underlying index, such as the S&P 500, a collection of 500 stocks intended to provide an opportunity for diversification and represent a broad segment of the market.

While the benchmark index does follow the market, as an owner of an FIA, your money is never directly exposed to the stock market. You invest an amount of money (premium) in return for growth potential based on the returns of a linked market index (e.g., the S&P 500 Index), and protection against negative returns of the same linked market index. Fixed index annuities were created during the mid-1990s, a time of tremendous stock market growth around the globe. They were positioned as an alternative to both fixed rate annuities and CDs. Index-linked returns will depend on how the index performs but, in general, the rate of return for an indexed annuity does not fully match the positive rate of return of the index to which the annuity is linked.

Bob and Connie retired in 2017. They both worked in corporate America and wanted to move to Tennessee to enjoy favorable weather, lower taxes, a small-town atmosphere, and their favorite pastime, golf. Things were good. Then came the pandemic in 2020. Their portfolio took a severe hit. Since they were drawing down income from their portfolio, they were concerned about the long-term ramifications of a stock market decline. Their financial advisor advised them not to change the portfolio. That turned out to be good advice because the markets recovered quickly and saw gains in 2020 and again in 2021.

Then in 2022, with war in Ukraine, soaring inflation, and political chaos caused by mid-term elections, the markets took a drastic turn downward. They sought a second opinion and were introduced to Witt Financial Group by friends who were our clients. What a shock when they found out the enormous risk in their portfolio. Our analytics report showed they could lose substantial capital in a market downturn like we saw in 2008 and temporarily in 2020.

During our discovery meeting, we discussed their goals and objectives. In the design meeting, we discussed an appropriate mix of equities and bonds based on their risk tolerance. We also introduced Bob and Connie to fixed index annuities (FIAs). By adding FIAs to the portfolio, we have introduced a new level of protection. Their income bucket includes FIAs to draw out income over the next ten years, effectively reducing sequence of return risk. It also allows the opportunity for money in their growth bucket to grow potentially without regard to sequence of return risk. We look at FIAs in a simple way. When stock market indexes rise, your equity portfolio and index-linked FIA will perform well. When market indexes fall, equities will suffer while FIAs will offer protection against loss.

Registered Index Linked Annuity (RILA)

Ronnie and Susan had been retired for ten years and had benefited from the strong stock market from 2010 to 2021. They wondered if markets could sustain this growth. They wanted to lessen their exposure to stocks, but were not willing to accept low fixed rates of CDs. They chose to reposition a percentage of their portfolio to a Registered Index Linked Annuity (RILA).

A RILA is a contract with an insurance company. It is a deferred long-term savings option that limits exposure to downside risk and provides the opportunity for growth, based on the performance of an index or indexes. It may offer more growth potential than a fixed-indexed annuity but less potential return and less risk than a variable annuity.

With RILAs, you accept a level of risk in exchange for higher upside potential than a MYGA or a FIA.

What registered index-linked annuities offer:
- A level of protection from market downturns: The money you place into your registered index-linked annuity will be partially protected from market downturns based on the level of protection you select.

- Opportunity for growth: Your money can grow based on the performance of an index or indexes.
- Tax advantages: The value of your annuity grows tax deferred, meaning you won't pay taxes on any growth until you make a withdrawal.

Most registered index-linked annuities offer a mix of term lengths, which is the amount of time you'll be allocated to your chosen combination of protection and growth potential. At the end of each term, you'll have the opportunity to make new selections. These types of annuities have surrender charge schedules (early withdrawal penalty) that go along with the length of term.

Annuities tend to get a bad rap in the press. Stocks and bonds are the predominant choice for pre-retirees, then when they retire, they lessen their equity exposure and up their exposure to bonds. That has worked well for decades, but look at 2022: stocks *and* bonds took a beating, so we can no longer assume that the stock/bond portfolio will always work. When you combine the protection of insurance products alongside stocks and bonds, it makes for a well-diversified retirement portfolio. A well-rounded retirement portfolio could include some or all of the following assets: stocks, bonds, mutual funds, ETFs, fixed annuities, FIAs, and RILAs.

Annuities aren't for everyone but it is important to understand how they work. Then you can make an informed decision. Sure, you can go for it on every par five regardless of conditions. But it could be wise to consider all of your options. It worked for Zach Johnson in the 2007 Masters!

*

---

* Annuities can play an important role in a portfolio but may not be appropriate for everyone. Before purchasing an annuity, it is important to understand the details of the product. A perfect financial product does not exist. Stocks may have a substantial upside but also may carry a significant downside. Annuities may offer downside protection, but that protection may come with a cost. A multi-year guaranteed annuity is a long-term product that may not be a good fit for everyone; it is not insured by the FDIC,

―――――――――――――――

it may offer limited liquidity; early withdrawal or surrender charges may apply, and the interest rate may not keep pace with inflation. A fixed index annuity is a long-term product that may not be a good fit for everyone; it is not insured by the FDIC, it may offer limited liquidity, early withdrawal or surrender charges may apply, protection of principal can limit interest or other earnings, and participation rates, caps, spreads and other factors to calculate earnings can change annually. A registered index linked annuity is a long-term product that may not be a good fit for everyone, it is not insured by the FDIC, it may offer limited liquidity, early withdrawal or surrender charges may apply, additional advisor fees may apply, and loss of principal exists if the negative return of a chosen index is in excess of the protection level selected.

CHAPTER 8

Estate & Legacy

In our practice, we devote a significant portion of our time to matters of estates. That doesn't mean drawing up wills or trusts or putting together powers of attorney or anything like that. After all, we're not estate planning attorneys. But we are financial professionals, and what part of the "estate" isn't affected by money matters?

We've included this chapter because we have seen many people do estate planning wrong. Clients, or clients' families, have come in after experiencing a death in the family and have found themselves in the middle of probate, high taxes, or a discovery of something unforeseen (often long-term care) draining the estate.

We have also seen people do estate planning right: clients or families who visit our office to talk about legacies and how to make them last, and adult children who have room to grieve without an added burden of unintended costs or the stress that stems from a family ruptured because of inadequate planning.

We'll share some of these stories here. However, we're not going to give you specific advice, since everyone's situation is unique. We only want to give you some things to think about and to underscore the importance of planning ahead.

You Can't Take It With You

When it comes to legacy and estate planning, the most important thing is to *do it*. We have heard people from clients to celebrities (rap artist Snoop Dogg comes to mind) say they aren't interested in what happens to their assets when they die because they'll be dead. That's certainly one way to look at it. But we think that's a very selfish way to go about things—we all have people and causes we care about, and those who care about us. Even if the people we love don't *need* what we leave behind, they can still be fined or legally tied up in the probate process or burial costs if we don't plan for those. And that's not even considering what happens if you become incapacitated at some point while you are still alive. Having a plan in place can greatly reduce the stress of those responsibilities on your loved ones; it's just a loving thing to do.

Documents

There are a few documents that lay the groundwork of legacy planning. You've probably heard of all or most of them, but we'd like to review what they are and how people commonly use them. These are all things you should talk about with an estate planning attorney to establish your legacy.

Powers of Attorney

A power of attorney—or POA—is a document giving someone the authority to act on your behalf and in your best interests. These come in handy in situations where you cannot be present or, for durable powers of attorney, even when you are incapacitated (due to a medical condition, for example).

It is important to have powers of attorney in place and to appoint someone you trust to act on your behalf in these matters. Have you ever heard of someone who was incapacitated after a car accident, whether from head trauma or being in a coma for weeks—sometimes months? Do you think their bills stopped coming due during that time? We like our phone company and our bank, but neither one is about to put a moratorium on sending us bills, particularly not for an extended or interminable period. A power of attorney would have the authority to pay your mortgage or cancel your cable while you are unable.

You can have multiple POAs and require them to act jointly.

What this looks like: Do you think two heads are better than one? One man, Chris, significantly relied on his two sons' opinions for both his business and personal matters. He appointed both sons as joint POA, requiring both their signoffs for his medical and financial matters.

You can have multiple POAs who can act independently.

What this looks like: Irene had three children with whom she routinely stayed. They lived in different areas of the country, which she thought was an advantage; one month she might be hiking out West, the next she could enjoy the newest off-Broadway production, and the next she could soak up some Southern sun. She named her three children as independently authorized POAs, so if something happened, no matter where she was, the child closest could step in to act on her behalf.

You can have POAs who have different responsibilities.

What this looks like: Although Luke's friend Claire, a nurse, was his go-to and POA for health-related issues, financial matters usually made her nervous, so he appointed his good neighbor, Matt, as his POA in all of his financial and legal matters.

In addition to POAs, it may be helpful to have an advanced medical directive. This is a document where you have pre-decided what choices you would make about different health scenarios. An advanced medical directive can help ease the burden for your medical POA and loved ones, particularly when it comes to end-of-life care.

Wills

Perhaps the most basic document of legacy planning, a will is a legal document wherein you outline your wishes for your estate. When it comes to your estate after your death, having a will is the foundation of your legacy. Without one, your loved ones are left behind, guessing what you would have wanted, and the court will likely split your assets according to the state's defaults. Maybe that's exactly what you wanted, as far as anyone knows, right? Because even if you told your nephew he could have your car he's been driving, if it's not in writing, it still might go to the brother, sister, son, or daughter to whom you aren't speaking.

However, it may not be enough just to have a will. Even with a will, your assets will be subject to probate. Probate is what we call the state's process for determining a will's validity. A judge will go through your will to question if it conflicts with state law, if it is the most up-to-date document, if you were mentally competent at the time it was in order, etc. For some, this is a quick, easily-resolved process. For others, particularly if someone steps forward to contest the will, it may take years to settle, all the while subjecting the assets to court costs and attorney's fees.

One other undesirable piece of the probate process is that it is a public process. That means anyone can go to the courthouse, ask for copies of the case, and discover your assets. They can also see who is slated to receive what and who is disputing.

It's also important to remember beneficiary lines trump wills. So, that large life insurance policy? What if, when you bought it fifteen years ago, you wrote your ex-husband's name on the beneficiary line? Even if you stipulate otherwise in your will, the company that holds your policy will pay out to your ex-spouse. Or how about the thousands of dollars in your IRA you dedicated to the children thirty years ago, but one of your children was killed in a car accident, leaving his wife and two toddlers behind? That IRA is going to transfer to your remaining children, with nothing for your daughter-in-law and grandchildren.

That may paint a grim portrait, but we can't underscore enough the importance of working with a skilled estate planning attorney to keep your will and beneficiary lines up to date as your life changes.

Trusts

A trust is set up through an attorney and allows a third party—or trustee—to hold your assets and determine how they will pass to your beneficiaries. Many people are skeptical of trusts because they assume trusts are only appropriate for the fabulously wealthy.

However, a simple trust will likely cost $1,500 to $2,500 if prepared by an attorney. Fees can be higher for couples.[52] But a trust can help you avoid both the expense and publicity of probate, provide a more immediate transfer of wealth, avoid some taxes, and provide you greater control over your legacy.

For instance, if you want to set aside some funds for a grandchild's college education, you can make it a requirement he or she enrolls in classes before your trust will dispense any funds. Like a will, beneficiary lines will override your trust conditions, so you must still keep insurance policies and other assets up to date.

---

[52] Rickie Houston. smartasset.com. "How Much Does It Cost to Set Up a Trust? https://smartasset.com/estate-planning/how-much-does-it-cost-to-set-up-a-trust

Like any financial or legal consideration, there are many options these days beyond the simple "yes or no" question of whether to have a trust. For one thing, you will need to consider if you want your trust to be revocable (you can change the terms while you are alive) or irrevocable (can't be changed; you are no longer the "owner" of the contents). A brief note here about irrevocable trusts: Although they have significant and greater tax benefits, they are still subject to a Medicaid look-back period. This means, if you transfer your assets into an irrevocable trust in an attempt to shelter them from a Medicaid spend-down, you will be ineligible for Medicaid coverage of long-term care for five years. Yet an irrevocable trust can avoid both probate and estate taxes, and it can even protect assets from legal judgments against you.

Another thing to remember when it comes to trusts, in general, is even if you have set up a trust, you must remember to fund it. In our combined thirty-five years of experience, we've had numerous clients come to us, assuming they have protected their assets with a trust. When we talk about taxes and other pieces of their legacy, it turns out they never retitled any assets or changed any paperwork on the assets they wanted in the trust. So, please remember: a trust is just a bunch of fancy legal papers if you haven't followed through on retitling your assets.

Taxes

Although charitable contributions, trusts, and other tax-efficient strategies can reduce your tax bill, it's unlikely your estate will be passed on entirely tax-free. Yet, when it comes to building a legacy that can last for generations, taxes can be one of the heaviest drains on the impact of your hard work.

For 2023, the federal estate exemption was $12,920,000 per individual and $25,840,000 for a married couple, with estates facing up to a 40 percent tax rate after that. Currently, the new estate limits are set to increase with inflation until January 1,

2026, when they will "sunset" back to the inflation-adjusted 2017 limits.[53] And that's not taking into account the various state regulations and taxes regarding estate and inheritance transfers.

Another "frequent flyer" tax concern: retirement accounts.

Your IRA or 401(k) can be a source of tax issues when you pass away. For one thing, taking funds from a sizeable account can trigger a large tax bill. However, if you leave the assets in the account, there are still required minimum distributions (RMDs), which will take effect even after you die. If you pass the account to your spouse, he or she can keep taking your RMDs as is, or your spouse can retitle the account in his or her name and receive RMDs based on his or her life expectancy. Remember, if you don't take your RMDs, the IRS will take up to 25 percent of your required distribution (10 percent if corrections are made in a timely fashion).

You will still have to pay income taxes whenever you withdraw that money. Provisions in the original SECURE Act dictate that anyone who inherits your IRA, with few exceptions (your spouse, a beneficiary less than ten years younger, or a disabled adult child, to name a few), will need to empty the account within ten years of your death.

Also—and this is a pretty big also—check with an attorney if you are considering putting your IRA or 401(k) in a trust. An improperly titled beneficiary form for the IRA could mean the difference of thousands of dollars in taxes. This is just one more reason to work with a financial professional, one who can strategically partner with an estate planning attorney to diligently check your decisions.

---

[53] Katherine Keating. Foley. February 13, 2023. "Increased Gift and Estate Tax Exemption Amounts for 2023."
https://www.foley.com/en/insights/publications/2023/02/increased-gift-estate-tax-exemption-amounts-2023.

CHAPTER 9

Why Retirement is Different for Women

Debra sat at the conference room table, tears streaming down her face. In front of her was a stack of unopened envelopes. She apologized for being unprepared. William, her beloved husband of forty years, had passed away after a long illness. He had always taken care of the finances, and while she believes she is financially well off, she feels caught off-guard by the enormity of the situation.

In our experience, it's more likely to be a woman than a man in that chair across from us in the conference room. Women have often embraced different roles than men as workers, wives, mothers and daughters. They are more apt to take on roles as caregivers. Women, in general, have not been intimately involved in the investing process, but that dynamic is changing quickly. Women are now being called on to be the Chief Financial Officer, or CFO, of the family's wealth, along with all of her other roles.

The world is constantly changing. And, for women, *your* involvement in *your* financial future is crucial. You can and you will take charge. Join me as we explore ways for you to become your family's CFO.

Be Informed

While there are many factors affecting women's financial preparation for retirement, we cannot emphasize enough that the decision to be informed, to be a part of the conversation and to be aware of what is going on with your finances, is absolutely paramount to a confident retirement.

With all couples, there is almost always an "alpha" when it comes to finances. It isn't always men–for many of our coupled clients, the woman is the "alpha." Half of households also say decisions about savings and investments are shared equally.[54]

Couples sometimes have their first real conversation about money and investing in our office. The important thing about having these conversations isn't where, it's when...and the best "when" is today.

A woman once commented to us that to get the conversation rolling, she asked her husband "to teach me how to be a widow." Perhaps that sounds grim, but she said it spurred a dynamic conversation. They spent a day, just one part of an otherwise dull weekend, going through everything relating to their family finances, i.e., income, investments, taxes, health care and legacy planning. They spent ten years together after that. When he died, she was prepared. She did not feel the enormous anxiety that all-too-many widows have because they were unprepared for this transition.

We met one couple, we'll call them Jim and Karen, and became their financial advisor. They had a wonderful marriage, three children, and ten grandchildren. Jim had always handled the investments. Karen rarely attended a strategy meeting, until one day, she did. She caught me in the hallway and said, "My husband is having some health issues, and I will be attending every meeting going forward."

---

[54] Megan Brenan. Gallup.com. January 29, 2020. https://news.gallup.com/poll/283979/women-handle-main-household-tasks.aspx

Her husband was a proud man, and she asked that we not say anything about his health just yet. The next year, we met several times. Then we received a call one day from Karen. She said they were moving to an assisted living facility because Jim had developed signs of dementia.

We visited several times, and each time we had great conversations. Then one visit, it was apparent that Jim was going downhill fast. He died a few months later.

The first time Karen came to the office after his death, she cried and said, "I've never handled the investments. Now I'm being forced to." She continued, "I don't want to mess this up because Jim has done such a good job accumulating money and investing it and then working with you. I'll never forgive myself if I mess this up!"

That day, we began a study course. We taught her about stocks and bonds, about financial planning for her future and about legacy planning for her loved ones. We taught her investment principles, but she took it a step further by reading and studying. Within a year, she was like a "pro" in our strategy meetings.

Karen was forced to take over the responsibility of managing the family wealth. And take it over she did. She took charge, and she did it well. I'll never forget a comment she made in a strategy meeting: "I'm so happy because I know Jim would be proud of what I have accomplished!"

Did You Know?

According to David Bach in "Smart Women Finish Rich," 80% of men die married, while 80% of women die widowed.[55] Let that sink in for a second.

The average woman lives seven years longer than the average man. So guess what? It's not a question of will I manage the family's financial affairs, but when?

---

[55] David Bach, Smart Women Finish Rich. 2009. Crown Publishing Group.

Taxes

One of the often unexpected aspects of widowhood is the tax bill. Many women continue similar lifestyles to the ones they shared with their spouses. This, in turn, means continuing to have a similar need for income. However, after the death of a spouse, taxes will be calculated based on a single filer's income table, which is much less forgiving than the couple's tax rates. With proper planning, your financial professional and tax advisor may be able to help you take the sting out of your new tax status.

More Health Care Needs

In addition to the cost of living for a longer lifespan is the fact aging, plain and simple, means more health care, and more health care means more money. Women are survivors. They suffer from the morbidity-mortality paradox, which states women suffer more non-fatal illnesses throughout their lifetime than men, who experience fewer illnesses but higher mortality.

Women have been found to seek treatment more often when not feeling well and emphasize staying healthy when older, according to studies.[56] So survival is on the side of the woman. However, surviving things, like cancer, also means more checkups later in life.

Caregiving

Of the 53 million caregivers providing unpaid, informal care for older adults, 61 percent are women. Among today's family caregivers, 61 percent work and 45 percent report some kind of

---

[56] advisory.com. July 22, 2020. "Why do women live longer than men? It's more complicated than you think." https://www.advisory.com/en/daily-briefing/2020/07/22/longevity

financial impact from providing a loved one care and support.[57] In addition to the financial burden created by caregiving responsibilities, women devote an average of 5.7 hours each day to duties such as housekeeping and looking after loved ones.[58] So then, when can women find the time to focus long and hard on financial matters?

Unfortunately, the impact and hardships created by traditional roles for women typically do not account for Social Security benefit losses or the losses of health care benefits and retirement savings. This also doesn't account for maternity care, mothers who homeschool, or women who leave the workforce to care for their children in any way.

We don't repeat these statistics to scare you. Estimates typically place the monetary value of unofficial caregiving services across the United States at around $150,000,000,000 ($150 billion) or more. Yet, we think the emotional value of the care many women provide their elderly relatives or neighbors cannot be quantified. So, to be clear, this shouldn't be taken as a "why not to provide caregiving" spiel. Instead, it should be seen as a call for "why to *prepare* for caregiving" or "how to lessen the financial and emotional burden of caregiving."

Women Becoming a Force in Investing

According to a 2021 Women and Investing study by Fidelity Investments, an analysis of more than five million Fidelity customers over the last ten years reveals that, on average,

---

[57] caregiving.org. 2020 Report. "Caregiving in the U.S. 2020."
https://www.caregiving.org/caregiving-in-the-us-2020/
[58] Drew Weisholtz. Today. January 22, 2020. "Women do 2 more hours of housework daily than men, study says."
https://www.today.com/news/women-do-2-more-hours-housework-daily-men-study-says-t172272

women outperformed their male counterparts by forty basis points, or 0.4 percent.[59] Are women better investors than men?

From our perspective, women tend to ask more and better questions. Thoughtful questions lead to more knowledge and ultimately better decisions. Better decisions lead to better results. Women tend to embrace the financial planning process and seek to collaborate with financial advisors on tailored strategies that fit their value system. And this is key: they develop a plan, then passionately follow that plan. Long-term success often is achieved by this simple strategy.

Women tend to be more risk-averse. Women tend to stay calm during volatile times. Women are more interested in building wealth as opposed to a get-rich-quick scheme. Whether women are born with it or develop it over time, they possess an innate behavior trait that all great investors have: they invest with their head and their heart. The head takes care of the intellectual aspect and the heart takes care of the emotional side.

Whatever the reason, women are becoming a force in investing. They are taking on the role of CFO of their family and doing a remarkable job.

When It All Comes Together

We met Joanna when she was a young lady, just sixty-eight. Her husband, Richard, had passed away a few years earlier at the age of seventy. She was suddenly called upon to be the Chief Financial Officer (CFO) of the family finances, even though she had no prior experience. We'll never forget that first meeting without Richard. She said, "Do I have enough money? Am I going to be OK?" Even though she felt unprepared, she was eager to engage in the investment planning process. So, we

---

[59] Fidelity.com. October 7, 2021. Women and Investing Study. www_fidelity com/documents/about-fidelity/Fidelity Investments Women Investing Study 2021.pdf

designed a comprehensive income plan with predictable income sources to cover expenses. Then, we worked on an investment plan that was tailored to her specific needs and risk factors. She began working with a local CPA firm. We introduced ideas to mitigate the risk of future long-term health care expenditures. We recommended she work with an estate planning attorney to update the family trust. One day in the office, she remarked, "I did it!" Joanna did it and so can you!

Joanna was the very definition of a successful woman, wife, mother, and grandmother. And now, for the first time in her life, she was in charge of her family finances. She was accomplishing something that seemed insurmountable just a short time ago. By gaining clarity on her financial situation, she was able to, once again, pursue new adventures. Anything Joanna wanted to do really came as no surprise to us because of her vibrant and indomitable spirit. Several years after becoming a widow, she popped into a strategy meeting and asked, "Do I have enough money for a big trip?"

We said yes, and asked where she was going. She said, "My daughter and her husband live abroad, and I'm going to the United Arab Emirates and Abu Dhabi and will be gone for two months."

We asked, "Are you traveling alone?" To which she replied, "Of course!" Nothing would deter her passion, or her desires to join her daughter on a once-in-a-lifetime excursion.

Joanna's inspiring story, and how she embraced retirement and the opportunities it presented despite the loss of Richard, can give all women something to look forward to. She became CFO of the family wealth and did a phenomenal job. Joanna took what life gave her and made the most of it. She passed away at the age of ninety-one and left not only a monetary inheritance to her family but also a legacy of love and adventure.

CHAPTER 11

Finding a Financial Professional

As a father and son, we consider ourselves blessed to have such a close relationship, both in and out of the office. It may be rare for a son to consider his father his best friend, but that's the case for us. In fact, Mark was the best man in Jordan's wedding.

Both of us had an interest in finances at a young age but took different paths to arrive where we are today. Mark spent seventeen years in corporate America, rising up the ranks to become a vice president at a public company. The job had its perks, but eventually Mark wanted something different that allowed him to prioritize his family over climbing the corporate ladder.

A long-time mentor suggested he engage in the financial services industry, and an in-depth personality test concurred. Of all the professions, the one that aligned best with Mark's interest was financial advisor. So in 2000, Mark began his journey in the financial services industry. In 2011, he made the decision to form a Registered Investment Advisory (RIA) firm and truly be independent. He considers it one of the best professional moves he's ever made.

Jordan frequently hung around the office as a kid, absorbing the basics of investments, and more importantly, seeing how his dad was able to help people with their finances. His upbringing led to an immediate interest in the financial world, but before joining his father's firm, Jordan first pursued another dream.

Baseball was one of Jordan's passions, and an internship with the Johnson City Cardinals allowed him to be close to the game, while holding onto his hopes of one day managing a club. When his boss handed him a check at the end of the summer for $500, his first thought was, "This is great!" Then he did the math and realized he made just $2 an hour!

Later that summer, his boss asked him for a favor. "The gentleman who's usually the mascot isn't here today," he said. "Will you step in and wear the costume?"

Being an intern, Jordan dutifully put on the bird costume to run the bases with kids and hand out pizzas. When he took off the costume and wiped off the sweat, he considered it a defining moment. He called Mark that night and said, "When I graduate, I want the opportunity to join you."

Fortunately, he had taken several finance and business classes at East Tennessee State University. The Monday after Jordan graduated, he was working alongside his father in the office, where he has remained ever since.

Mark has run the business for decades and continues to find joy helping clients sort out their finances, but whenever the day comes that he'll retire, he'll do so knowing his son will carry on the family business for decades to come.

The 1980s and 1990s brought about the greatest bull market run in the history of the world, creating wealth for investors far and wide. Then the dot.com market decline hit, just as Mark was entering the industry. He saw how investors, at no fault of their own, bore the brunt of a brutal three-year market decline. Markets came back strong, but from late 2007 to early 2009, the world was devastated by the Great Recession. Fortunes were wiped out during this tumultuous period

This is why it's so critical today to work with a trusted financial professional. Markets are unpredictable. The older we get, the more certainty we like in retirement planning.

When Mark and Jordan look back over their careers, they realize how many lessons they have learned, certainly during bull markets, but more importantly during bear markets. Kind of like the old saying from Franklin D. Roosevelt, "A smooth sea never made a skilled sailor."

Tips on finding the right advisor:

1. Experience—The first thing to consider when choosing a financial advisor is the level of experience they have in financial markets. Has the advisor worked through multiple cycles of the economy? Have they faced the exuberance of a bull market and the fear of a bear market? The learning experience of both comes in handy when guiding clients through various stages of economic growth or decline.

2. Communication Skills—Ever spoken to a doctor with a great bedside manner? One who can take complex issues and make them seem simple? Likewise, have you ever spoken to a doctor with a bad bedside manner? One who complicates already complicated issues, and you walk away feeling worse? Your financial advisor needs to be able to take complex matters and relay that information to you in an understandable fashion.

3. Transparency—While you don't have to be a financial expert yourself, you do need to understand your investments. An advisor must be clear on what they recommend and why. An advisor must also be clear on how they are compensated. Are they paid a fee, a commission, or a combination of both?

4. Independent Thinking—An advisor must give you honest advice based on their knowledge and experience and lead you toward financial independence. An advisor

must tell you what you need to hear, not only what you want to hear.

Meet Elizabeth and Michael:

Elizabeth and Michael grew up in Southern California, began dating in high school, and were married soon after graduating from Stanford University. She worked as an information security analyst. He worked as an architectural engineer. They raised three children. Once the children had settled into their careers, Elizabeth and Michael began to explore places to retire. Their search led them to Crossville, Tennessee.

They attended an informational workshop held by Witt Financial Group and requested a strategy meeting to discuss their retirement plans. Elizabeth was the "alpha" when it came to the family finances. She described herself as a knowledgeable investor. However, she was terrified about retirement. She and Michael saved considerable money during the accumulation phase in qualified plans and brokerage accounts. But the idea of drawing down their assets in the decumulation phase frightened her. Would they have enough money if they lived into their nineties or beyond? How would they cope with escalating health care costs? And, would they be able to leave an inheritance to their children? All great questions and she wanted answers. So, we set an initial strategy meeting in our office.

Elizabeth specified their goals. They wanted to pay off their home and be debt-free in retirement. They wanted to explore guaranteed income products, invest in the markets for long-term growth, be tax-efficient, plan for potential health care expenditures, and leave a legacy of not only money, but also wisdom, to their children and grandchildren.

We listened closely as they shared their dreams and goals. After the initial strategy meeting, we met a second time to collaborate on the financial plan. It was important to work together and craft a plan specifically designed for them. In the third strategy meeting, we put the final touches on the plan and welcomed them to the Witt Financial Group family. Elizabeth thanked us for our patience and attentiveness while making the process easy to follow and understand.

In 2020, the COVID-19 pandemic rocked stock markets across the world. During a March 2020 strategy meeting via telephone, Elizabeth thanked us for the call, and added that she was not worried about retirement. "We thoughtfully put together a plan," she said, "and we're sticking to the plan!" She remarked how she and Michael enjoyed their lives in Tennessee and were planning vacations to Napa Valley and Italy.

When we see Elizabeth and Michael at the office or an event, she is quick to give us a hug and say "thank you" for designing their retirement plan. They no longer worry about money. They have an attitude of joy and contentment. They are living out their dreams. Elizabeth and Michael even discovered a new pastime; they play golf three times a week in the Golf Capital of Tennessee!

MARK & JORDAN WITT

About the Authors

H. Marcus "Mark" Witt
Founder & President

Mark Witt is an author of two books, *Successonomics* and *Bogey-Free Retirement*, the talk radio host of *Smart Money Radio*, and a fierce proponent of free market capitalism. Mark's *Smart Money Radio* show airs weekly on Talk Radio 96.3, 105.7 The Hog, 93.3 The Ranch, and Spirit 101.9. Mark's no-nonsense, hard-hitting approach on air helps investors to better understand financial markets and develop a disciplined approach to retirement planning. An industry leader and public speaker, Mark has shared his message of global investing with thousands of people around the country.

Mark credits May 28, 1970, as a turning point in his life. On that night, he attended a Billy Graham crusade at Neyland Stadium and asked Jesus Christ to be his Lord and Savior.

Mark and his wife, Glenda, have been married for forty years. They have two sons, Jordan and Grayson. Jordan graduated from East Tennessee State University and is Vice President of Witt Financial Group. Grayson, a beautiful child with disabilities, is an active participant in Special Olympics.

Jordan Witt
Vice President & Investment Advisor Representative

Jordan strives to provide comprehensive financial planning strategies to pre-retired and retired individuals, helping them achieve total wealth optimization and reliable income sources in retirement.

Jordan's decision to enter the financial services industry was inspired by his father, Mark. Now, as a leader of Witt Financial Group, Jordan works hard to help establish a clear purpose for his clients' financial futures and provide the insight and guidance necessary for them to reach their goals.

Due to the success of his weekly radio show, "Smart Money Radio," Jordan has become a sought-after speaker on progressive personal finance and retirement planning strategies in Tennessee.

Jordan graduated from East Tennessee State University with a Bachelor of Science. He is an Investment Advisor Representative, passed the Series 65 securities exam and is a licensed insurance agent in Tennessee. He is also a Chartered Retirement Planning Counselor™ (CRPC®).

Jordan and his wife, Katherine, have two daughters, Emma Katherine and Eliza Jordan, and son, Barrett Robert. Jordan attends Central Baptist Church in Crossville and is an avid golfer—he's proud to live in the Golf Capital of Tennessee. He enjoys spending time at the lake and spending quality time with friends and family. Jordan is also a fan of Tennessee football and enjoys cheering on the Volunteers.

91 Hwy 70 E, Suite 102
Crossville, TN 38555

Phone: 931.484.4911
Email: info@wittfinancialgroup.com
Web: wittfinancialgroup.com

Made in the USA
Columbia, SC
27 March 2025